PROFESSOR CAROL'S
A History of
Early Sacred Music

From the Temple through the Middle Ages

BY CAROL B. REYNOLDS, PH.D.

Silver Age Music, Inc.
Plano, Texas

Published in the United States by Silver Age Music, Inc.
Plano, Texas

Library of Congress Cataloguing-in-Publication Data
ISBN 978-0-9819990-5-0
Carol B. Reynolds, author
A History of Early Sacred Music
From the Temple Through the Middle Ages

First U.S. Edition

© 2016 Silver Age Music, Inc.

Printed in the United States of America

About the Course

The course takes the student through the development of early sacred music, beginning with the first references to music in the Old Testament and ending at the dawn of the Renaissance. The historical record of these times is sparse, and music historians must rely on a variety of secondary sources to reconstruct the music. By studying the general history, the theology and philosophies of the times, as well as contemporary descriptions of the music, the student will gain insight into the nature and purposes of the music and how it was employed in Christian worship.

The course stresses mastery of certain terms and familiarity with key historical figures. It also emphasizes knowledge of geography. The terminology allows us to discuss certain features of the music—some of which will presumably be encountered for the first time—and to track their development. Geography and general history provide the necessary context. Of course, the music itself is our ultimate focus. We encourage students to listen to the music repeatedly to gain familiarity with it, but the larger goal is to understand the music in relation to its purpose in a specific time and place.

The main instruction for this course comes in the form of video lessons from Professor Carol on the enclosed DVD set. Additional instruction in this text expands on the video, and we have also included a glossary and "Who's Who" for easy reference. Assignments that help teachers and students explore the subject in more detail can be found in a separate "workbook" along with a quiz for each unit. The answer key for quizzes can be found in the back of the workbook.

This course is designed to fit within one semester. It contains 12 Units, each comprised of a separate video, a chapter in this text, and unit assignments in the workbook. Each unit can normally be completed in one-week increments. You may work at any pace you wish, however. By pursuing some of the assignments and outside materials in greater depth, the course may spread across an entire academic year.

If you have any questions or wish for assistance with the course, please contact Professor Carol: carol@professorcarol.com.

THEOLOGICAL PERSPECTIVE

Many people who contemplate embarking on a study of sacred music want to know whether it fits their own religious perspective. Is it biblical? Is it Protestant or Catholic? Is it open to all religious perspectives? These are fair questions to which we respond with a few basic observations.

First, the authors of the course are unapologetically Christian, and we presume that most of those who take the course will be Christian as well. But our study of sacred music does not look solely at what happened within the church walls. It deals also with how music within the church was shaped by numerous external and secular factors, including political and social history, economics, and technology. We discuss the historical purposes of music in the church, but we do not present theological or sectarian arguments in favor of any particular doctrine or form of music. We acknowledge the Jewish roots of Christianity and emphasize the profound ways in which Christian chant and liturgy were shaped by Jewish traditions. Our discussions of theology and philosophy are intended to explain the reasons music developed as it did, not to persuade the student to any particular point of view.

Second, this study ends with the Middle Ages, before the Protestant Reformation, and so it does not take on the issues that surround that division. It deals with the history of a mostly united Christian Church—a history shared by Protestants and Catholics. We devote one unit to Eastern Orthodoxy and the ways in which its chant followed a different path from Western musical tradition.

Much of the course focuses on the Latin Mass and the Daily Offices of Benedictine Monks. That focus reflects the reality of music history, and we have tried throughout to follow the dictates of history. The liturgy and the chant form the basis of our Western musical heritage. The great composers of the Common Practice Era (1600-1914), both Catholic and Protestant, understood and incorporated these liturgical forms: Bach, Handel, Mozart, Schubert, Liszt, Brahms, and many more. An understanding of the Mass and early chant is essential not only to the study of music in the Catholic Church today, but also to the study of Protestant hymns, the Anglican tradition, modern Praise worship, and many styles of secular music.

The course features a great deal of commentary from Benedictine monks who continue to sing the chant daily. They have a unique historical perspective. Their scholarship and generosity should be an inspiration to all. We also feature extensive commentary from classicists, medievalists, and musicologists from various religious perspectives. If we put them all in the same room together, we are confident they would engage in a spirited and charitable exchange of ideas that would enlighten all of us.

And that, in a sense, is what we have attempted to do in this course. We explore our common artistic heritage from several perspectives. That common heritage is a body of transcendent Christian art and music of indescribable beauty, and we believe it is the task of all Christians to honor and preserve it.

Acknowledgments

When we first began working on this course, we considered our options for gathering high-quality video from locations of historical significance. We travel frequently to Germany and other parts of Europe, something that is both a "perk" and a necessity to my work as a music historian. But we had never been to the Holy Land and doubted that our professional opportunities and schedule would ever take us there.

We were wrong. At the very moment I was contemplating our limited filming options, and while my husband was talking to legal clients on a conference call, I took a break and scanned my spam box. A spam box is a logical place to find junk emails with subject lines like "cruise and educational opportunity," right? After nearly deleting this particular email, I opened it—skeptically—to find what appeared to be a *bona fide* offer to speak on behalf of The Smithsonian. The destination? Rome, Athens, Jerusalem, and points in between—just the places we needed for a study of the Temple and early Christian liturgy.

My husband waived off any interruption as I jumped up and down beside his desk, so I did what any prudent person would do and accepted the offer without waiting to consult him or ask the first question! Call it Divine Providence or a happy coincidence, I thank God for opening this door. And, of course, I do thank The Smithsonian and Sadie McVickers of Smithsonian Journeys who kept the travel opportunities coming!

On that very trip we made connections with a marvelous group of musicians, scholars, and monastics. On one of the most magical days of our lives, we visited in Rome with a brilliant, witty scholar and master teacher of chant, Sr. (Dame) Margaret Truran. She astonished us by taking us privately down *underneath* the *Chiesa di Santa Cecilia* in Trastevere, right onto the actual excavated Roman streets and buildings where St. Cecilia lived as patron to the early Christians and, eventually, was martyred. On a return visit, we were able to conduct an interview with Sr. Margaret and profit from her advice.

We also were blessed by the expertise and unbridled enthusiasm of Jerusalem archeologist Yuval Edden. Touring the holiest sites in Jerusalem with him will always be a high point of our lives. (Thanks for the camel ride, Yuval.)

Another great opportunity for the course came later when we made contact with a group of Italian musicians and researchers known as Synaulia. If you ever saw the movie *Gladiator*, you've heard their vibrant Roman music performed on reconstructed period instruments. In particular we must thank Walter Maioli, Luce Maioli, and Ivan Gibellini. They also made arrangements for us to be able to film in a massive excavated Villa San Marco in Castellammare di Stabia, outside of Naples, that lies literally at the foot of Mount Vesuvius.

Equally critical to the course has been our connection with an ensemble of Italian singers known as *Ring Around Quartet*. Yes, it's a funny name for Italian singers who specialize in medieval and renaissance music. But when they created their ensemble as university students years ago, it was "hip" to come up with an English-language name, and it stuck. We cannot sufficiently express our gratitude to Vera Marenco, Manuela Litro, Umberto Bartolini, and Alberto Longhi for all that they did: for their music, their friendship, and for arranging a way for us to film inside the *Chiesa di Santa Maria Maddalena* in Camuzzago. Also, we want to thank their colleagues Aimone Gronchi, Maria Notarianni, Atsufumi Ujiie who brought their instruments for a day of filming together. Many thanks, too, to Salvatore Urso who served as our director in Camuzzago.

Far distanced from warm Italy, in northern Russia, gratitude goes to the singers of Terra Musica, an ensemble of Russian singers whom we filmed on the remote island of Kizhi. Their recorded music also appears in this course, and we will never forget their kindness.

Closer to home, we had the marvelous fortune to gain an association with the monks of St. Louis Abbey. Time spent with them has been invaluable. Our deepest gratitude goes to Abbot Thomas Frerking, Prior Gregory Mohrman, Prior Timothy Horner, and Fr. Bede Price. Their wisdom, joy *and* music have enriched and shaped many units of this course. In our several visits to the monastery, we shared stories and ideas and chanted the Daily Offices with them. In addition to their friendship, we gained an abiding appreciation of the monastic life.

Those who know the work here at Professor Carol immediately realize that my husband, Hank Reynolds, has been a driving force behind the creation of this course. His theoretical and academic knowledge brought forth much of the prose for the text. No words are strong enough to describe the amount of videography and editing, creative design, and the wisdom he has brought to the process.

Appearing throughout the course are musicians, scholars, and specialists, without whom (to use the old phrase) this course would not exist. These include our favorite art historian Dr. Peter Mooz (well known to our students of *Exploring America's Musical Heritage* and *America's Artistic Legacy*); Professor and master organist Dr. Christopher Anderson; musicologist, composer, and violinist Dr. Michael Dodds; Professor of Philosophy Dr. John Trapani; and esteemed medievalist Dr. Jeremy Adams—all magnificent scholars and teachers *par excellence.* We're so happy, too, that we could interview Dr. Christopher Perrin, Classics scholar and valued colleague, and include his commentary in the course.

In the same vein, we appreciated the chance to spend time with Belgian archeologist and linguist Jacques Pauwels whose knowledge of the daily world in which Jesus dwelt was extremely helpful.

Others, behind the scenes served as much-needed consultants, including Fr. David Allen, Fr. Robert McBride, Rabbi Jack Segal, Abbot Philip Anderson, and my dearest long-time friend from our days at Leningrad Conservatory in the early 1980s, Valentina Kaniukova. Valentina also arranged for us the extraordinary opportunity to film at the Novodevichy Convent in St. Petersburg.

In short, there could be no course without all of these people and the opportunities afforded us to present their expertise. May their gifts and devotion enhance your experience as you travel through the journey of Early Sacred Music.

Table of Contents

1. Credo

The *Credo* (Creed) begins with a proclamation of our belief in one God. *Credo* (I believe) *in unum Deum* (in one God).

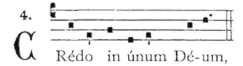

Rédo in únum Dé-um,

This statement stands at the heart of Christian and Jewish belief. For centuries, the Hebrew people proclaimed, "Hear, O Israel, the Lord our God, the Lord is one." (*Sh'ma Yisrael Adonai Eloheinu Adonai E[x]ḥad.*)

The Credo is one of the parts of the *ordinary* of the Mass, meaning it is a component of the Mass that is said or sung "ordinarily"—in every Mass. Other parts of the Mass change from day to day or with the season of the year, and these parts are known as the *proper*. We will explore the overall structure of the Mass later on, paying particular attention to the five parts of the *ordinary*:

Kyrie eleison
Gloria
Credo
Sanctus et Benedictus
Agnus Dei

For now, you just need to know that some parts of the Mass are constant (*ordinary*), some parts change to fit the specific occasion (*proper*), and the Credo is part of the *ordinary*.

We begin with the *Credo* not because it is the first chant, or the first part of the Mass, or even the first thing we come to chronologically in our history. We begin with the *Credo* because it points out some important features of Gregorian chant, and chant is one of the main focal points of early sacred music. It also helps us give a broad overview of some of the important historical developments that will mark our study.

A Paradigm of Sacred Music

Gregorian chant can be seen as a paradigm for the sacred music of Christianity. Chant had been used for centuries by monastics as the basis of their daily life of prayer and sung worship. We find the chant in the oldest manuscripts containing musical notation (dating from the 10th century), but we are not limited to that evidence. Musicologists have other ways of discovering the nature of music both before and after the development of notation.

Gregorian chant reflects centuries of practices with certain aspects of the chant presumably having roots in ancient Jewish practices. Later in this course we will see how the Gregorian melodies were used in the late Middle Ages and Renaissance to build increasingly elaborate sacred compositions. And we will see how these melodies were used as a foundation for music in the baroque and classical periods and are being used by composers living today.

Chant

The term "chant" refers to a way of singing. One primary feature of chant is that it is *non-metrical*. Most of Western music has a metrical pulse, rhythmic groupings of 2, 3, 4, or sometimes 6 beats per measure. We often call this metrical pulse the "beat," the thing we respond to when we dance or tap our feet. Chant, however, has a different kind of rhythm. It does not set up a regular pattern of pulses. Instead, it follows the natural rhythm of the text, the rhythm that would occur if you were simply speaking the text. The sacred text takes priority over the melody, so chant melodies follow the words, and the musical rhythm is made to fit the text rhythm.

To understand this better, consider the famous Christmas carol "It Came Upon a Midnight Clear." If you simply read the text, you would use a very different rhythm from the melody of the carol. The melodic rhythm, in triple meter, conforms to a metrical pulse built on groupings of three. Speaking the words to the rhythm of the carol sounds very unnatural as you bend the speech pattern to fit the musical meter. In chant, however, the words do not bend to fit the music; the music bends to fit the words.

Chant frequently involves singing a line of text on a single note (pitch) or singing most of the line on a single note with a slight melodic gesture at the end. It may also move from note to note much as a modern melody might. To the extent chant uses multiple pitches, those pitches tend to be close together. They fit in a limited range that is easy to sing. The melody moves most often to adjacent pitches (like adjacent white keys on the piano or notes in a scale) and rarely "leaps" to non-adjacent pitches.

Consider two familiar melodies: "Yankee Doodle" and "Somewhere Over the Rainbow." The melody of "Yankee Doodle" moves mostly (not always) to adjacent pitches. In contrast, the melody of "Somewhere Over the Rainbow" contains wide leaps.

MONOPHONY AND MONODY

The chant of the early Christian church was also *monophonic*, meaning that it consisted of a single, unaccompanied melodic line. We frequently give monophonic music the name *monody*.

Please note that the word "monody" can be used to describe different things in music. It does not refer solely to religious chant, although, for the purposes of our course, it will.

For example, an entire style period of singing in European late renaissance/baroque vocal music is described as "monody." In this era, the term refers either to a new style of popular music that developed in the late Renaissance and led to both a new type of music called opera (in Italian) and to a body of popular short Italian songs written for a single voice and featuring the newest poetry. The vocal line in both cases was accompanied by instruments. These are important developments in late renaissance and baroque music, but they happened centuries after our story of Early Sacred Music and are unrelated.

Additionally, much folk music across the world is sung by a single, solo voice. Indeed, a folk song conveyed by solo singer, without any kind of accompaniment, is one of the purest ways for folk songs to be learned, mastered, performed, and transmitted to the next generations.

Monody does tend to be used as a term for the singing voice. A single, unaccompanied melody line sounded by solo flute, clarinet, oboe, or trumpet, is, indeed monophonic, but musicians generally use other terms when discussing instrumental music.

SAINT LOUIS ABBEY

The video for this unit shows a service of vespers at St. Louis Abbey where Benedictine monks sing worship services multiple times each day. Gregorian chant is always a part of these services, although some are sung in English rather than Latin. The monks at St. Louis Abbey founded the St. Louis Priory School (on the grounds of the monastery) where Latin is an essential part of the curriculum. Many of the monks teach at the school.

THE AESTHETICS OF CHANT

People have many different reasons for singing the chant in worship – because of what it is or what it does. Historians study it, preserve it, and attempt to recreate performances that show how the music was sung in earlier times. Other people seem to "re-discover" the chant from time to time. Have you noticed that recordings of Gregorian chant are now being sold in places like coffee shops and that vocal groups who specialize in medieval music are touring the world? Chant has a special appeal. People today find it therapeutic, even those who have no particular interest in its religious application. It speaks to people at a fundamental level, and there are good reasons why it holds such a prominent place in the overall history of music. If you are tempted to take its single-line simplicity as indicating that the chant is somehow primitive, think again. What seems simple in any art form often results from a profound elegance.

ORAL TRADITION

Music of the early church was not written down at first. It was learned and passed on through "oral transmission." A singer would hear the music and commit it to memory. Chant would be sung frequently in services of the early church and taught to succeeding generations. As Christianity spread across diverse geographic regions, communication was difficult and infrequent. Consequently, a unified body of chant was difficult to achieve, and it was bound to vary somewhat, sounding different depending on where you heard it. The chant sung in Milan (known as *Ambrosian chant*) would differ from the chant sung in Rome, for example, and other variations on the chant melodies and texts would be found across the vast territory of the Christian world. What we call Gregorian chant comes from an effort to bring those various styles into conformity.

WHO WAS GREGORY AND WHY IS HIS NAME CONNECTED TO CHANT?

Gregorian chant takes its name from Pope Gregory I (c. 540 – 604). Being in Rome, Gregory would surely have known and practiced the Roman form of chant, and when chant later became standardized across Europe, it followed predominantly the Roman form. But there is little evidence to connect Gregory with the standardization of the chant, much less to attribute specific melodies to him. This may comes as a surprise to you, since Gregory's name has become almost inseparable from chant. But Gregory's role in creating chant is a matter of legend. Consider the chronology of events: To standardize the musical liturgy into what we now know as Gregorian chant, the music had to be carried great distances. Monks at each monastery had to learn to sing the same chant that was sung in other monasteries. The development of a reliable system of musical notation was critical to this effort. Oral transmission alone could not accomplish this kind of standardization. Whatever Pope Gregory's contribution to the musical practices of the Church may have been, it predated the development of musical notation by centuries.

The term "Gregorian chant" is thus a rather imprecise designation of a standardized liturgy that occurred only well after Gregory's lifetime. Standardization is the key. How did a wide variety of musical practices taking place across the vast territory of the Christian world become this unified thing—something we can name as Gregorian? We see the evidence of it in the earliest manuscripts to have survived the ravages of time and come down to us, namely manuscripts from the 10th and 11th centuries. In these manuscripts, scholars note a remarkable uniformity of the repertoire. We credit this development as beginning, not under Pope Gregory, but under two worldly figures who followed in the 8th and 9th centuries: Pepin and his son, Charlemagne or, if we pull his name apart, Charles Magnus, or Charles the Great. We will have a lot to say about them later in this course.

Under Charlemagne, who consolidated vast territories of today's Europe under his rule, the Roman rite became the standard form and was spread throughout Europe. Charlemagne would be responsible for many important developments in writing and manuscripts that would help spread knowledge rapidly and reliably across Europe, and his efforts would have an enormous influence on the history of music.

THE HISTORICAL RECORD

How durable is music? The question of durability arises in all of the arts with each artistic medium facing its own peculiar issues. Arts that exist in a tangible medium, such as stone or canvas, can survive for a very long time if properly cared for. Because they are embodied in a single object, however, they are uniquely susceptible to destruction by fire, flood, or earthquake. Books can be faithfully reproduced in copies, although this was a very laborious process until recently (historically speaking). Perhaps you think of music as being rather like books, capable of being reproduced reliably on paper. But written musical notation captures only an outline of the music. The actual sounds could not be captured until the invention of the gramophone in 1877.

So keep in mind that we have no musical notation for much of the period we are studying in this course, and obviously we have no recordings from the time. When musical notation comes along, it tells us many things but still leaves many questions unanswered.

LANGUAGE

Gregorian chant uses Latin texts almost exclusively. You many think of Latin as ancient and wonder why people would use an old and dusty language in church. But Latin was a relative newcomer to the Christian church.

The Old Testament had been written in Hebrew, but by the time of Jesus, Hebrew was somewhat like Latin today, an old language used primarily in religious services. Jesus would have known the ancient Hebrew texts, but his native tongue was Aramaic. Aramaic had become the predominant language of Assyria in the 8th Century B.C. and later of Babylon. It spread through much of the Middle East along with the Babylonian Empire. Alexander the Great's vast conquest in the 4th century B.C. solidified Greek as the language of knowledge and as a language of commerce among various peoples. St. Paul, a Jew and Roman citizen, wrote his epistles in Greek, and many of the early Church Fathers worked out the tenets of the Christian faith in Greek.

So what about Latin? The Romans had, by the time of Jesus, taken over all of the territory bordering the Mediterranean. Latin was therefore the language of the political rulers. When Constantine established Christianity as the religion of the Roman Empire in 325 A.D., Latin came to the fore. The old Latin versions of scripture (*Vetus Latina*), existing in various fragmented forms, were superseded in the late 4th century by St. Jerome's more authoritative Latin translations (what would become the standard Latin Bible or *Vulgate*). A few decades later when the Western half of the Roman Empire collapsed and Europe fell into chaos, the knowledge that could be preserved was preserved in Latin. Latin was spoken in Europe by educated people throughout the period we call the Dark Ages. So while Latin today may seem like a barrier to understanding, in the Dark Ages it was a bridge—a language that connected otherwise isolated regions to each other and that connected the small, educated class to the accumulated knowledge of the Empire. Latin would die only as the secular forces of the Renaissance brought regional dialects to prominence through literature.

2. Jerusalem

The view of Jerusalem is the history of the world. It is more; it is the history of earth and of heaven. –Benjamin Disraeli

A study of the earliest history of music requires us to address a central question: How do we know what we think we know? Archeological evidence can be interpreted different ways, and scholars may disagree on what the evidence means, but at least there are stones and relics to examine. But sounds? Musical sounds that disappeared into the air seconds after they were sung, thousands of years ago? How do we reconstruct those?

EVIDENCE OF MUSIC

Musicologists have various sources and methods that they can use to draw conclusions about the nature of ancient Jewish music. Like archeologists, they can study the material objects that a culture has left behind, including its architecture, environment, and artifacts (archeological evidence). What instruments were used to produce sounds and in what kind of space did that sound resonate? They can study the form and structure of the surviving arts – literature, painting, sculpture – to gain insight into patterns and motifs that animated the thinking of the time (morphological evidence). They can use what they know of oral tradition, how it functions, its strengths and weaknesses. The political, economic, and geographical circumstances will have a strong influence on how reliably the oral tradition is passed on and the likelihood that it might spread. They can examine the writings of the time, which may discuss music-making or things related to music-making, and they can make certain inferences from this (philological evidence). Old Testament accounts provide some of the best evidence of music-making and liturgical practices.

None of these provides a complete picture of music in ancient times, but all of them can shed some light on the subject and help to reconstruct the music.

INSTRUMENTS

Archeological evidence can be particularly useful in the study of instrumental music, and much of the music described in the Old Testament is instrumental. Some instruments made of durable materials survive. Such instruments can be replicated and played, so we can know the sounds available to a musician of the time and what the instrument was capable of playing. Biblical accounts tell us how the instruments were used. They tend to emphasize the exuberance of the music. Musical instruments would have had a special place in the ancient world where the concept of sound was much different.

VOCAL MUSIC

Ancient vocal music is more difficult to reconstruct. Rabbinical writings in the first centuries after Christ are very helpful. Although these writings postdate Jewish worship in the Temple, they draw on a very strong oral tradition.

SUMERIANS AND EGYPTIANS

We have good evidence of music going back to ancient Sumeria. This civilization in Mesopotamia lasted possibly more than two millennia and seems to have sprung out of nowhere. It may cause you to rethink your conception of "ancient" as the demise of Sumeria in 2004 B.C. predates Classical Greece by some 1600 years. How advanced was it? The Sumerians apparently invented written language, and much more:

> Examples of Sumerian technological inventions include the wheel, copper, bronze, the arch, sailboats, lunar calendars, sundials, saws, chisels, hammers, rivets, sickles, hoes, blue (bitumen), swords and scabbards, harnesses, armor, musical instruments (the lyre and harp), chariots, the kiln, sun-dried and kiln-fired bricks (mixed

with straw to give them greater strength), the pottery wheel, printing, plows, metal cooking post, and (last but not least) beer.[1]

Archeologists have uncovered cuneiform tablets describing diatonic tuning systems and the notation of music. Deciphering that information accurately and reconstructing the actual sound of the music remains a daunting task for musicologists. But one can now listen to what scholars believe to be Sumerian music on YouTube. The important Sumerian city of Ur, near the mouth of the Euphrates, is identified by many scholars as Ur of the Chaldees, the home of Terah and his son Abram. [Genesis 11:27] The Sumerians had a longstanding conflict with their neighbors the Akkadians, but with whom they shared a language and many traditions. The Akkadians were later known as Babylonians.

More early evidence of music comes from ancient Egypt in the third millennium B.C. We know about the instruments played and something about how the music was structured. And from visual depictions, we can learn how the music was used.

> The ancient Egyptians did not notate their music before the Graeco-Roman period, so attempts to reconstruct pharaonic music remain speculative. Representational evidence can give a general idea of the sound of Egyptian music. Ritual temple music was largely a matter of the rattling of the sistrum, accompanied by voice, sometimes with harp and/or percussion. Party/festival scenes show ensembles of instruments (lyres, lutes, double and single reed flutes, clappers, drums) and the presence (or absence) of singers in a variety of situations.[2]

It lies beyond the scope of this course to delve deeper into the music of Sumeria and Egypt. As the reader encounters references to music in the book of Exodus, however, it may be helpful to bear in mind that music was not new. And after years of captivity in Egypt, the Hebrew people most likely would have absorbed many Egyptian musical practices. But also their music would have had deep cultural roots, and it would have been a defining feature of both sacred and secular events.

---

[1] Sumerian Shakespeare. http://sumerianshakespeare.com/21101.html.

[2] Kelsey Museum, "Music in Ancient Egypt," University of Michigan,http://www.umich.edu/~kelseydb/Exhibits/MIRE/Introduction/AncientEgypt/AncientEgypt.html.

THE LEVITES

Priests of the Tabernacle[3]

The twelve tribes are Israel are said to have descended from the twelve sons of Jacob. Thus, Levi, the third son of Jacob and Leah, is the founder of the tribe of Levi, the *Levites*. The Levites were set aside as the priestly tribe, and Moses and Aaron were both descendants of this tribe. Aaron and his sons thus received the role of priests. [Exodus 28] When the Israelites entered Canaan, the Levites were the only tribe not given land because "the Lord the God of Israel himself is their inheritance." [Deuteronomy 18:2]

---

[3] Illustrators of the 1897 *Bible Pictures and What They Teach Us* by Charles Foster. https://commons.wikimedia.org/wiki/File:Foster_Bible_Pictures_00722_Priests_of_the_Tabernacle.jpg

As the priestly tribe, the Levites were placed in charge of the Ark of the Covenant and the Tabernacle.

> But thou shalt appoint the Levites over the tabernacle of testimony, and over all the vessels thereof, and over all things that belong to it: they shall bear the tabernacle, and all the vessels thereof; and they shall minister unto it, and shall encamp around about the tabernacle.
>
> And when the tabernacle setteth forward, the Levites shall take it down: and when the tabernacle is to be pitched, the Levites shall set it up: and the stranger that cometh nigh shall be put to death. [Numbers 1:50-51]

The Levites retained these duties when the Ark of the Covenant was moved into the Temple. Among the Levites who served in the Temple were musicians and temple guards.

TEMPLE HISTORY

Abraham was told to go to the land of Moriah and offer his son Isaac as a sacrifice on one of the mountains. [Genesis 22:2] Tradition identified this site as Mount Moriah, and the city of Jerusalem would be built nearby. King David captured Jerusalem from the Jebusites in about 1000 B.C., and it became the City of David. David then purchased the site of Isaac's near sacrifice just north of the City of David from a Jebusite named Araunah and placed an altar there. [2 Samuel 24] That became the site of the Temple. David brought the Ark of the Covenant to Jerusalem but was not permitted by God to build the Temple because he was a warrior king, and so the Temple was built on the summit of Mount Moriah by David's son, Solomon. [2 Chronicles 22]

The original Temple built by King Solomon dates to the 10th Century B.C. Scripture describes its construction in detail. [1 Kings 5-7] The Ark of the Covenant was housed in the innermost chamber, the Holy of Holies. Solomon's Temple stood as the focal point of Jewish worship until 587 B.C. when the Babylonians destroyed the Temple and took the Hebrew people into exile. [2 Kings 24]

The Babylonian Empire itself fell to the Persians in 539 B.C., and Cyrus the Great permitted the Jews to return to Jerusalem and rebuild the Temple. This Second Temple, built on the original site, was dedicated in 515 B.C. [Ezra

5] Little information survives concerning the Second Temple. It was presumably built at the same site and in the same dimensions as the First Temple but lacked the grandeur.

Grandeur came in abundance when King Herod greatly expanded the second Temple in the 1st Century B.C., some 500 years later. Although the changes made by Herod were significant, mostly occurring between 19 B.C. and 9 A.D., Herod's Temple is still generally considered a continuation of the Second Temple because the sacrifices were never interrupted by Herod's construction. People sometimes refer to it as the "second, second Temple." It is Herod's Temple that Jesus would have known. Herod's Temple stood for only a short time before it was destroyed by the Romans in 70 A.D.

The Second Jewish Temple. Model in the Israel Museum.[4]

---

[4] Photo by Ariel (CC BY 3.0) https://commons.wikimedia.org/wiki/File:Second_Temple.jpg

If you visit the Temple in Jerusalem today, you will see the outer walls of Herod's construction. You also see the large structure within the walls known as the Dome of the Rock, a Muslim structure that sits on the place where the Holy of Holies once stood. Although the Israelis recaptured this part of Jerusalem in the Six-Day War of 1967, access to the Temple Mount remains under Muslim control. Many Jews go to the Western Wall (sometimes called the Wailing Wall) to pray because it is the spot along the outer walls that is closest to the Holy of Holies.

PERSONAL REFLECTION ON VISITING JERUSALEM

Everyone says it: visiting the Holy Land will change you. They are not wrong. The experience of wandering through the ancient streets of Jerusalem causes a great deal of rethinking. Most significant is the jolting realization that so much of what one has read about in the Bible happened *right here*. And we can still see much of it! But the scope is so small. I envisioned the City of David as a towering kingdom on a mountain, whereas it's actually a modest hill with dwellings clinging to it.

The same with the Garden of Gethsemene. Of course it's riddled with noisy traffic and overrun by tourists today. But instead of a maze of endless fields, it's an intimate space, not far from the city walls. No wonder Jesus was disappointed when his disciples repeatedly dozed off, because he was surely within earshot.

Lasting impressions for me included the realization that some of the dingy kiosks in the crowded streets have been in the same family for centuries. Or realizing that Jesus probably drank the same utterly delicious pomegranate juice I was drinking, albeit not squeezed by electric juicers.

The politics of today, of course, overwhelms everything. A quiver of anxiety runs through every street. The unsolvable issues that tear apart the sons and daughters of Abraham create impressions that do not fade once the visit is over. You do take Israel home with you. That's what people mean, I think, when they speak of "visiting the Holy Land" as a life changer. It remains a vivid frame of reference forever, bringing point after point in the Bible to life, starting with the Temple of Solomon.

The Destruction of the Second Temple

Jesus predicted the destruction of Jerusalem as he approached the city on Palm Sunday.

> For the days shall come upon thee, that thine enemies shall cast a trench about thee, and compass thee round, and keep thee in on every side, and shall lay thee even with the ground, and thy children within thee; and they shall not leave in thee one stone upon another; because thou knewest not the time of thy visitation. [Luke 19:43-44]

In 70 A.D., after a Jewish uprising against Rome, the city was laid waste on a shocking scale by the Romans. The collapse of Jerusalem was preceded by conflicts between the Zealots and other factions of Jews. When the Romans besieged the city, those conflicts grew. Anyone attempting to escape Jerusalem risked being killed by either the Zealots within the walls or the Romans outside the walls. Mass starvation spawned brutality of neighbor against neighbor. When the Romans finally broke into the city, they burned the Temple, demolished the city walls, and slaughtered the population. The eyewitness Josephus chronicles the gruesome events in *The Wars of the Jews; or the History of the Destruction of Jerusalem*. This first Jewish-Roman War would not end officially until the last Jewish stronghold of Masada was taken by the Romans in 73 A.D.

The Jewish-Roman wars would continue with the Kitos War (115-117) and the Bar Kokhba Revolt (132-136). The latter may have been sparked, although evidence is sketchy, by Emperor Hadrian deciding to rebuild the Temple and then dedicating it to Jupiter. Once the Jews were defeated in this last uprising, Hadrian banned the practice of Judaism. He burned the sacred scrolls on the Temple mount and prohibited Jews from entering Jerusalem, which he had renamed Aelia Capitolina. Christians were barred from Jerusalem as well.

Time and Place

We say that music is always tied to time and place; it does not occur in a vacuum. Music has a function beyond its ability to entertain. It necessarily reflects that purpose along with the circumstances of its creation and performance. When the Hebrew people ceased their desert wandering and moved into a fixed place, when the Temple replaced the tent, the circumstances of worship changed and we should expect that the music accompanying and facilitating that worship to change with it. A sense of continuity might have been extremely important: the sacred obligations and rituals had the same purpose. But the acoustics had certainly changed. And more importantly, the ethos that surrounds a nomadic people no longer exerted its influence.

After the Jewish-Roman Wars, the Jews were again without a Temple and without a homeland. Would the diaspora Jews develop a different music? Almost certainly, while at the same time they may have clung to the remnants of their cultural life more tenaciously than ever.

And what of Christian music? It would not be formed in Jerusalem, in the shadow of the Temple, but would take to the road. It would take root in the synagogues of disparate towns where St. Paul would preach, as many of the early Christians were Jews who understood monotheism and the historical context of the Gospel. And Christian music would encounter the world of the Gentiles, shaped by the philosophies and language of the Greeks and ruled by the Romans.

3. Into What World?

After the Resurrection, the first Christians, the apostles, continued to attend Jewish services in the Temple and in synagogues. [Luke 24:52-53, Acts 3:1, Acts 9:20] They directed their preaching to their fellow Jews. Peter's first public pronouncement was directed to the men of Judea, his fellow Jews, and he laid out for them how the prophecies had pointed to Jesus. [Acts 3:14-36] The apostles viewed the Christian faith as consistent with Judaism and as an extension of it.

Christian liturgy developed accordingly. It did not throw out the well-established Jewish practices, but rather added to them. We see this clearly in what we know of the earliest Christian liturgical practices and in what continues to this day: a liturgy of the word very much following the pattern of the synagogue services, followed by the Eucharist, the specifically Christian addition to that service.

Prior to the destruction of the Temple, Jerusalem remained the center of Christianity. But by then Peter and Paul had both gone to Rome and been martyred under Nero (r. 54-68). The church was growing outside of Jerusalem and finding many Gentile converts. The devastation of Jerusalem in 70 A.D. followed by the banishment of Jews and Christians from Jerusalem by Hadrian in 136 ensured that Christianity would flourish, if at all, in the Greek and Roman world.

MUSIC IN THE SYNAGOGUE

We have seen that music within the Temple was boisterous and accompanied by numerous instruments. The synagogue service moved away from the use of instruments and to a more subdued style of worship. Several factors have been advanced as explanations. The synagogue grew out of the Babylonian Exile and separation from the Temple, so its initial purpose was not so much one of worship but instruction. Babylonian culture may have exerted an influence. The return from Babylon saw the beginning and eventual domination of rabbinic influence, and the rabbis may have limited or prohibited the use of instruments. Although the playing of an instrument would have been permitted on the Sabbath, tuning or repairing an instrument could be forbidden acts of work. Moreover, the celebratory nature of instruments might have been deemed inappropriate for Jews living under foreign domination. The *Jewish Encyclopedia* explains:

> As the part of the instruments in the Temple musical ensemble was purely that of accompaniment, and the voices could have given an adequate rendition without accompaniment, the absence of instruments from the synagogue in no way modified the system of the song itself. This presented little that to modern ears would appear worthy the name of melody, being, like the Greek melodies which have been deciphered, entirely of the character of a cantillation; that is, a recitation dependent on the rhythm and sequence of the words of the text instead of on the notes of the tune, and influenced by the syntactical structure of the sentence instead of by the metrical form of the musical phrase.[5]

The music of the synagogue is described here as having a significant similarity to Greek melodies: the rhythm conforms to the syntactical rhythm of the text and is not metrical. Early Christian chant, as we saw in Unit 1, would adopt this same defining approach. The non-metrical speech rhythm of Gregorian chant had a long and varied progeny.

The synagogue service typically included two scripture readings, one from the Torah and the second from one of the Prophets. The readings from the Torah were arranged so that the entire Torah would be read twice every seven years. These readings were cantillated by a reader using standard melodic formulas.

The congregation would participate in the recitation of psalms guided by a *precentor* (cantor). Certain responsorial patterns might be used. The precentor might intone a half verse of the psalm with the congregation repeating it. In the Hallel [Psalms 113-118], the precentor might intone the first half verse, which would then be repeated by the congregation, and then the precentor would intone the entire psalm with the congregation repeating the first half verse as a refrain. Other responsorial patterns might be used

---

[5] Jewish Encyclopedia, "Music, Synogogal." http://jewishencyclopedia.com/articles/11241-music-synagogal.

along with occasional antiphonal singing in which one half of the congregation would respond to the other.

We see these same patterns adopted in Christian liturgy for the readings of scripture and the recitation of the Psalms. Antiphonal singing was employed more frequently in the Eucharist, recalling the scene in Isaiah 6 in which the seraphim call back and forth to each other, "Holy, Holy, Holy is the Lord of Hosts."

The earliest Christians drawn from Judaism continued in the practices and observances in the Temple and synagogues. They added to this an observance of the Eucharist. This often took place on Sunday, the day of the Resurrection. Sunday in Jewish tradition began at sundown on Saturday, and the Eucharist could thus take place on Saturday night after the Jewish Sabbath services earlier in the day.

Numerous events drove a wedge between the Jewish and Christian practices, or diminished the Jewish influences. Without analyzing the import of each event, we can at least take note of them. For one, traditional Jews viewed the Christian sect as a heresy and persecuted its adherents beginning with St. Stephen. The destruction of the Temple eliminated the focal point of Jewish worship, dispersing it among the synagogues, and this obviously affected the Jewish Christians as well. Many Jews believed that the leader of the Bar Kokhba revolt, Simon bar Kokhba, was the Messiah; the Christians did not adhere to this view and thus did not support the Jewish uprising. When the Christians and Jews were both banned from Jerusalem by Hadrian after the Bar Kokhba revolt, their centers of influence moved in different directions.

When St. Paul took the Gospel to the Gentiles, Christianity encountered a different set of circumstances. Its new adherents did not have Jewish traditions and were not receptive to taking on the obligations of Judaism. St. Paul argued forcefully that the Gentiles could be fully Christian without circumcision, and the controversy led to wider debate on how Christians would interpret Mosaic law. However one analyzes Paul's theology, it is apparent that the Gentiles entered into Christianity with a different perspective from that of their Jewish brethren.

CHRISTIANITY IN ISRAEL, GREECE, AND ROME

As the early Christians moved out of Jerusalem and spread throughout the Roman Empire, what cultural world did they encounter? How was the music of the early church influenced by the arts of Rome and Greece?

Christ gave his disciples the Great Commission, to "make disciples of all nations, baptizing them in the name of the Father and of the Son and of the Holy Spirit, and teaching them to obey everything I have commanded you." [Matthew 28:19-20] At the time, Jewish communities had already been scattered into regions far from Israel. The Assyrian and Babylonian captivities began the Diaspora. Many Jews chose to stay in their land of captivity rather than return home and had settled in other cities. The city of Alexandria, for example, had a significant population of Jews. Richard Fletcher points out an often overlooked aspect of Judaism at that time.

> As an offshoot of Judaic stock, early Christianity was heir to the proselytizing zeal of its parent. Accustomed as we are to a merely self-perpetuating style of Judaism which was brought about by subsequent centuries of Christian and Islamic religious repression, it is easy to forget that the Judaism of the Hellenistic world was an evangelizing faith, and not one by any means conceived as being exclusively for adherents who were of Jewish ethnicity.[6]

Greek remained the language of urban and commercial centers around the Mediterranean, and Christianity took root initially in the urban centers: Alexandria, Corinth, Ephesus, Thessalonica, as well as Rome. We have to look at the cultural and artistic environment of the time to find clues to the music and to think about what forms of music the early Church might have encountered and what forms it may have adopted.

Christian missions to the pagan Gentile population found success initially among the less educated, those on the lower rungs of the economic ladder. Such people were less invested in the prevailing culture and beliefs of Greek and Roman society, and they might be persuaded that Christianity offered them rewards that their earthly existence could not. But as Christianity took root and spread, the more learned took notice. The better educated needed a different form of persuasion. They required the guidance of scholars, trained in logic and knowledgeable about pagan beliefs, who could debate and

---

[6] Richard Fletcher, *The Barbarian Conversion* (Univ. of California Press, 1997), 13-14.

explain why they should convert to Christianity. St. Paul would begin that process on the Aeropagus (Mars Hill) in the shadow of the Parthenon in Athens. [Acts 17:16-34]

Much of the intellectual life of the early church followed this formula, absorbing Greek education and philosophy and presenting the Faith with the skills of classical rhetoric and logic. Among the church fathers strongly influenced by Plato and other classical thinkers were Clement of Alexandria (c. 150-214), Origen (c. 184-253), and Eusebius (c. 265-340). Philosophy, the seeking of truth through reason, would complement theology, the study of revealed truth. Philosophy would be used to demonstrate the reasonableness of the faith.

MUSIC THEORY AND PHILOSOPHY

We tend to think of music theory today as the nuts and bolts of music—chord progressions, key signatures, notation—things that have a practical application for performing musicians. For the ancients, music theory reached far beyond such pragmatic concerns. It included the study of aesthetics and sociology and even the ordering of the universe. And while we may think of music theory as a specialized corner within the larger world of music performance and listening, the ancients would have seen it quite differently. Skilled musical performance would have been viewed as a specialization within the larger world of music. Music theory would not be called "music theory," or "music philosophy," or "aesthetics." It would be called simply "music." Music was included in the Liberal Arts not for the purpose of turning out good kithara players, but for turning students into good scientists and mathematicians and even theologians.

A few examples will have to suffice for our study.

Pythagoras, known for the Pythagorean Theorem that we all encounter while learning math, is also known as the first music theorist. Writing in the 5th century B.C., he explained the mathematical principles behind music, pointing out that musical intervals can be expressed as simple ratios (octave 2:1, perfect fifth 3:2, perfect fourth 4:3). These ratios can be seen easily in a length of vibrating string; cut its length in half (2:1), for example, and it will produce the same pitch an octave higher. Pythagoras went much further to explain the more complex aspects of tuning. His concept of *musica universalis* extended these musical principles to the movements of the sun, moon, and planets. These emit their own resonance that creates the "harmony of the spheres."[7]

Woodcut from *Theorica Musicae* by Franchino Gaffurio (1492)

Plato's philosophy followed that of Pythagoras in significant ways, but Plato's writings on music were not based on math. Plato was more concerned with the effects of music. Music, he argued in *The Republic*, could express virtues and vices and could encourage either virtues or vices in the listener. Certain musical modes therefore had to be treated with care and controlled or even prohibited. Aristotle subscribed to this view in his arguments concerning the place of music in education. Children should be taught music, he said, in a way that will make them good judges of music and not taught on instruments that will inflame the passions.[8]

---

[7] Pythagoras's work comes to us only through secondary sources, and so we speak here of ideas attributed to Pythagoras and his school of thought.

[8] Aristotle, *Politics*, Book 8, Chapter VI.

The Greeks had a sophisticated knowledge of the science of acoustics and a well-developed philosophy concerning the arts and the concept of beauty. Plato saw beauty as man's path to knowledge:

> Beholding beauty with the eye of the mind, he will be enabled to bring forth, not images of beauty, but realities (for he has hold not of an image but of a reality), and bringing forth and nourishing true virtue to become the friend of God and be immortal, if mortal man may.[9]

Plato's philosophy influenced early Christianity primarily through Plotinus (204-270) and the school of thought now called Neo-Platonism. It is through reading the Neo-Platonists that St. Augustine would reject the Manichean heresy and find his way to Christianity.

INTRODUCING SYNAULIA

Synaulia recreates the music of ancient Rome using archeological and iconographic evidence.

We filmed Synaulia at the Villa San Marco in Castellammare di Stabia, Italy. The villa overlooks the Bay of Naples with a stunning view of Mount Vesuvius. In 79 A.D., a catastrophic eruption of Vesuvius buried the villa along with the neighboring city of Pompeii. Archeologists have explored the site of Pompeii since 1748. Exploration of the Villa San Marco began in 1749 and continues today.

Synaulia works with The Vesuvian Institute in Castellammare. Using the archeological evidence, Synaulia recreates the sounds of ancient Rome. How can they do this? Much of their work focuses on studying the musical instruments of the time. Some instruments have been dug out of the ground intact or sufficiently intact to enable them to be replicated. Other instruments are depicted in visual art, on vases or frescos. These depictions tell musicologists not only about the construction of the instrument itself, but often about the manner in which it was played. They may show how the instrument was held, the position of the player's hands and how the weight of the instrument was borne. Musicologists may learn from such depictions

---

[9] Plato, *The Symposium*, Sec. 212

which instruments were used in combination. Through the careful study of all these factors, researchers gain an understanding of the array of sounds that likely would have resulted. The actual performances require certain inferences, but they provide remarkable insight into the soundscape of ancient Rome.

You may have already heard some of Synaulia's music. They did much of the soundtrack for the movie *Gladiator*. We spent several very memorable days with Synaulia's director, Walter Maoli, meeting him in Milan and traveling with him by train across Italy to Castellammare. He has a wealth of knowledge and shares it generously. We quickly discovered that Walter carries his flutes with him and is not shy about pulling one out and demonstrating his points wherever he may be, including in coffee shops and on trains. His daughter Luce shares his passion for music and hospitality, and we are most grateful to them both and the other members of their troupe for their contribution to this study.

ORAL TRANSMISSION

Almost everything can be accessed today in recorded or written form, or so it seems. We are accustomed to finding an objective, concrete record of most everything. So when we think about oral transmission as way to pass on important information, we may be tempted to discount its importance and to question its reliability, to put it in a suspect category – like hearsay or rumor. But even today, a great deal of information continues to arrive in our brains orally. We pay to hear people who are good speakers, we listen to the radio and download podcasts, and we favor the spoken word over the written word in numerous other ways. Information that is spoken carries a dramatic impact sometimes lacking in written prose.

Imagine that the information being conveyed to you orally is not merely data that can be accepted or rejected, not just someone's opinion, or the details of the coming sale at the supermarket. Instead, the thing being conveyed is the essence of your culture or instruction in matters of survival. Imagine that it comes in the form of engaging stories, rhymes, and songs. You might remember your early childhood, how much you learned, the melodies and stories you committed to memory before you were ever handed your first-grader reader. Much of that knowledge came to you through oral transmission and through dogged repetition, the kind of repetition children often insist on.

Oral transmission is a powerful source of knowledge. It relies on memory devices – melody, rhyme, repeated formulas – that imprint the information reliably. The nature of the information obviously matters. Data on a spreadsheet would not lend itself to being transmitted orally. On the other hand, music, even among those with no musical training, can be recalled in surprising detail, frequently down to the finest nuances.

Whole cultures were sustained for generations on the strength of oral transmission. Much of the Old Testament existed in oral tradition long before it was put in written form. It is a powerful method of communication, and the information passed on through oral transmission is essential in defining a culture.

Consider also how our modern ability to capture music in recordings and to broadcast those recordings to every part of the world has created a new form of oral transmission that is replacing written notation in many quarters. How many young people today gain some ability to play or sing music simply by listening to recordings without ever learning to read music?

4. The Roman Empire

In any study of the early Christian world, it is important to have a basic understanding of the Roman Republic and the Roman Empire along with an appreciation of Roman culture. Rome was a patriarchal society that placed a high value on family and tradition. Sculptures from the time frequently portray dignitaries not in some idealized form emphasizing youth and physical beauty (as the Greeks might have done), but as patriarchs—men whose status derives from seniority and accumulated wisdom.

Roman society was infused with a strong sense of civic duty and personal honor. It prized stability. While its history is full of episodes of political instability and shifting power, its longevity, both as republic and empire, and its military success demonstrate its strength and resilience.

When Greece fell to Rome in 146 B.C., Greek culture was absorbed into Roman life. Rome adopted much of what was fashionable in Greece: its art, architecture, literature, music, and even cuisine. Educated Romans learned both Greek and Latin. The mythological gods of Greece would receive Roman names.

The Romans were introduced to Greek philosophy in significant part through the works of Cicero (106 B.C. – 43 B.C.). Cicero was born into humble circumstances, but his skills as an orator and legal advocate propelled him to political prominence. Cicero is said to have turned Latin from a modest utilitarian language into a versatile literary medium capable of expressing abstract and complicated thoughts with clarity.[10]

---

[10] *Merriam-Webster's Encyclopedia of Literature* (1995), s.v. "Ciceronian period."

LITURGICAL CONTINUITY

Who were our witnesses for early liturgy? First, the group of people known as the Apostolic Fathers—people who had personally met and known either Jesus or his disciples. These included:

- Clement of Rome (d. 99 or 101), who, according to Irenaeus and Tertullian, was consecrated by St. Peter as bishop of Rome.
- Ignatius of Antioch (c. 35-c. 108), student of John the Apostle.
- Polycarp of Smyrna (69-155), who, according to Irenaeus and Tertullian, was a disciple of John the Apostle.
- Writers of the *Didache* (a collection of treatises dated anywhere from 50 A.D. to the early 2nd century)

After these, we have a group of patristic writers who wrote intensely to establish Christian traditions and defend Christianity against forces that would defeat it. These included:

- Justin Martyr
- Irenaeus of Lyon
- Clement of Alexandria
- Athanasius of Alexandria
- Tertullian
- Origen
- Cyprian of Carthage
- Ambrose of Milan
- John Chrysostom

Depending on your own religious education, the names of the church fathers may be familiar to you, or they could be wholly new. But they documented for us the development of issues of greatest importance to early Christians: Christianity's relationship with Judaism; the complex issue of deciding which writings (books) would become part of the accepted New Testament Canon; explanations of Christian tenets of faith (called apologetics today) and the need to achieve consistency of these tenets within the new faith, particularly in the Christianized Roman Empire.

These writers came primarily from Rome, Alexandria, Antioch, Carthage, Jerusalem, Milan, and Constantinople. Their writings, along with ancient tradition and archeological and artistic evidence, gives us our best understanding of early Christianity.

Additions to the Liturgy

Baptism

Arguably the most important new element of Christian worship was baptism. This was not a ritual cleansing which would be repeated on special occasions. This was Christian initiation. In this early Christian era, the sacrament often took place in house-churches, private meeting places secluded from officials. One of the most prominent house-churches in Rome belonged to a wealthy young woman named Cecilia. She is celebrated widely as the patron saint of music, but her story is far different from what that title would imply.

Eucharist

For the overall shape of Christian worship, and certainly for the story of music, the most critical aspect is the *Eucharist*, the Lord's Supper.

Evidence indicates that the Eucharist initially remained its own feast. It seems clear that Sabbath worship involved both the traditional form of service and a separate Eucharistic service as well. How and when these two elements were combined to become one continuous service—a service we soon will call Mass—has occupied many scholars.

As interesting as that research is, though, more important is to acknowledge that, even once joined, they remain two elements in liturgical structure. The *Catechumens*, those persons training and preparing to become Christians via Baptism, were welcomed into the first part of worship—the part inherited most directly from the Jews: the declamation of the word, the prayers, and the singing of psalms. Today this element broadly is known as the Liturgy of the Word and is sometimes described as the "teaching" segment of the liturgy. But Catechumens were excluded from the next element, the segment comprised of texts that prepare for the sacrament of Communion. And, technically, in strict liturgical traditions, they still are. Of course very few churches today actually escort unbaptized Christians out at this point in the service, but one may still find it occurring in certain practices.

So later in this course, as we follow the path that led to the creation of the full text of the Mass, remember that we are tracing the development of worship practices that were always characterized by continuity and a high degree of structure.

Daily Prayer

Another good example for how Christian worship evolved from Jewish tradition is the rotation of services for daily prayer. Evidence for these services also is found in early historical sources, particularly from the important source called the *Didache*.

We know that Christians were expected to pray, in fact not just twice, but three times a day. And, daily prayer had as its cornerstone The Lord's Prayer—certainly a cornerstone in the new Christian doctrine. But the standard for a rotation of daily prayer was set long before Christ or the record of the Lord's Prayer. The key to this again is the Scriptures. The patristic author Clement of Alexandria indicates that the 3rd, 6th, and 9th hours are proper for prayers, citing as biblical precedents passages such as Daniel praying three times a day [Daniel 6.10] or Peter praying at the 6th hour. The Scriptures contain references to prayers at midnight, too. These prescriptions will lead to midnight becoming one of the appointed "hours" for the Christian prayer services ultimately known as the Offices. And the Offices are particularly important because they are a showcase of texts that were sacred to the Hebrews: the Psalms.

Music

Where Was Music Used in Early Christian Worship?

- Intoned scriptural declamation. *Lectio solemnis*. This follows directly the traditions of Jewish cantillation, and we can assume the traditions had continuity. What is declaimed or cantillated? The Gospels, the Epistles, the Prophecies.

- Psalmody and Hymnody. We know there was strong emphasis on singing psalms and hymns. This is well documented in scripture and affirmed in the patristic literature. But the terms *Psalmos* & *Hymnosare* were used synonymously and interchangeably at times in the Scriptures and early patristic writings. [Eph. 5:19; Colossians 3:16] We can't find in early Christian worship an exact distinction until the 4th century when there will be specificity in how the terms are used. Even then, they still can mean different things depending on the region. We will find different practices as well. The Western Christian world will be inclined towards a more metrical delivery of text, where there is a regular pattern of pulses. The Eastern Christians will gravitate more towards a prosaic delivery (*pezos logos*) with rhythmic pulse generated completely by the text and not organized according to a pattern of beats. One thing we will see consistently in early Christian worship: the musical expression of psalms and/or hymns was always under suspicion for being too extravagant, or too metrical. At times, certain practices of singing could be withdrawn or prohibited.

- Direct Psalmody. This involves conveying the text of the psalm with a single precentor (cantor). As one of its strengths, it kept the traditions of psalmody accurate via strictures of oral tradition. Isidore of Seville in the early 7th century wrote, "Unless sounds are held in the memory of men, they perish since they cannot be written down."[11] Even this late in the first millennium, a rock-solid understanding of oral transmission was in effect.

- Responsorial Psalmody. Early Christians would have been familiar with this practice. A precentor would cantillate a psalm and people would have responded to each verse with a refrain, be it alleluia or another text perhaps taken from the psalm itself. This practice was long used in the Eastern church and can still be found today in monastic settings, about which we'll be speaking in an upcoming unit.

The language of worship in the Roman Empire, after Christ's death, was Greek. And the traditions and attitudes toward devotion were Jewish. Greek classicism had significant influence, and in other regions—Egypt for instance—different influences are intertwined. But Greek ideas still sculpted the budding liturgy.

The two earliest surviving Christian hymns are Greek, and they confirm this influence. The first is a beloved text, still used, called "O Gladsome Light" (from c. 150 A.D.). The second is a fragment of an actual hymn to the Trinity found on a fragment of papyrus excavated in an Egyptian town called Oxyrhynchus.

As informative as these sources are, they are not useful in reconstructing a tradition. The Oxyrhynchus Hymn, for example, has qualities that we would not have found in early psalmody. It is a specifically notated Greek melody using a specific Greek scale, with a largely pre-set classical Greek meter of anapestic dimeter. It has a large ambitus, or range of pitches. This would not

---

[11] Isidore of Seville, *Etymologies*, Ch. 15 §2

be the style in which we would expect to find the musical delivery of the Psalms, Gospel recitations, or prayers. (See the Assignment in this Unit for more on the Oxyrhynchus Hymn.)

FROM PERSECUTION TO FAVOR

Diocletian, known for the last great persecution of Christians in the Roman Empire, had rescued the empire from the Crisis of the Third Century. From 235 to 284, Rome came close to collapse, suffering through invasion, plague, economic depression, and civil war. Power resided with the army, which designated a succession of generals to be emperor. To become emperor, the generals promised rewards to the army, which prompted the army constantly to seek new emperors and new promises. Diocletian made radical changes. He greatly increased the size of the army, but more importantly he increased the size and reach of a vast administrative state with much more efficient methods of collecting taxes. And he solved, or thought he had solved, the problem of succession by creating the Tetrarchy.

The Tetrarchy divided the empire into East and West—a division that has endured ever since. But the Tetrarchy failed to provide for a smooth succession when Diocletion and Maxentius, co-emperor in the West, jointly abdicated in 305. Power struggles erupted, and Constantine emerged victorious in the West with his victory at the Battle of Milvian Bridge in 312.

Constantine, along with the emperor in the East, Licinius, issued the Edict of Milan in 313 giving legal status to Christianity but not making it the official religion of the empire. Constantine went further than mere toleration. He gave back property confiscated under Diocletian and exempted the church from taxation. The rate of conversions to Christianity increased with perhaps half the population being Christian by the end of Constantine's reign. Theodosius would make Trinitarian Christianity the official religion in 380. By the end of Theodosius's reign in 395, Christians represented as much as 90 percent of the empire.

After Constantine's defeat of Licinius, he chose Byzantium to be the new capital of the empire. Byzantium, which would be renamed Constantinople, was strategically located at entrance to Black Sea. From there the Roman army could be moved quickly to defend the frontier along the Danube or alternatively to the frontier with Persia.

The City of Rome had been the cultural and political center of the empire, but power and influence shifted to Constantinople. The Italian peninsula was left on the fringe, more isolated culturally, economically, and militarily. Romans in the 4th century, especially those in the East, might have thought that all was well and that Constantine had reestablished the stability and strength of the empire. But the Western half of the empire would fall to the Visigoths in the next century. The West would gradually lose touch with Greek and the accumulated knowledge that was bound up in that language. With the collapse of the political and social structures in the West, the Church would become the primary repository of knowledge.

5. Pray Without Ceasing

The rise of monasticism in the 4th Century took place as Christianity became the favored religion of Rome and, shortly thereafter, the official religion of Rome. Church and state were mingled with one another. But monastic life offered a refuge from the secularization and politics that were becoming more pronounced in the Church.

In the earliest form of monasticism, men went into the desert seeking isolation and a singleness of purpose. Our earliest example is St. Anthony (251-356) who lived an extraordinarily long life in harsh conditions. By escaping the complications of life in society and being alone with one's thoughts, one might hope to find a new and deeper understanding of God. It was a path that had been modeled by Jesus, John the Baptist, and indeed the Hebrew People. St. Anthony's decision to live alone in the desert was not new, but his dedication was inspiring. That inspiration reached many new followers once St. Athanasius (296-373) published his biography of St. Anthony.

The move from St. Anthony's model of the lone hermit in the desert to St. Benedict's Rule for monks living in community was an essential step in establishing the type of monasticism that could act as a center of learning. Only in community could the monks take up intellectual pursuits and the tedious work of preserving and disseminating books and manuscripts.

And so, although monasticism began in part as an escape from the excesses of Rome, it would become the chief preserver of the learning achieved by ancient Rome and Greece. It became the focal point for the intellectual life of the church and the repository of education and the arts throughout the Middle Ages. Monks would become the leaders of the church, its bishops and popes.

THE WRITINGS OF ST. AUGUSTINE

Of particular importance in informing the intellectual life of the church in the Middle Ages, and its spiritual direction, are the extensive writings of St.

Augustine of Hippo (354-430). We have many opportunities in this study to think about the fragility of historic sources—the frequent loss to fire or flood of manuscripts that existed in single, or very few, copies. The fire was at Augustine's doorstep. Vandals were destroying the North African city of Hippo as Augustine lay on his deathbed, and yet his writings were saved much to the benefit of future generations.

Augustine gives a detailed account of his own conversion in *The Confessions*, often considered the first autobiography. Raised by a Christian mother, St. Monica, and a pagan father, Augustine received an extensive education and was groomed for success in the secular world. After a period of subscribing to the Manichean heresy, he was introduced to the philosophy of Plato and neo-platonists such as Plotinus. There he discovered the intellectual foundation that led him back to Christianity, and under the tutelage of St. Ambrose in Milan, he completed his conversion and was baptized at age 33. While Augustine admired the example of St. Anthony and sought nothing more than a life of quiet contemplation, he would instead become Bishop of Hippo.

When Rome was sacked in 410, pagans assigned the blame to Christians, who, they claimed, had weakened the empire. In response, Augustine wrote *The City of God*—one of the monumental works of Christianity and Western Civilization. Augustine contrasted the earthly city with the heavenly city, and focused on the concept that man was a stranger (*peregrinus*) on earth.

> Here was an exacting standard for the Christian. He must become a peregrinus, an exile or pilgrim, make of his life a peregrinatio, a pilgrimage, cutting loose like a monk from the worldly ties that bind and accepting instead the liberating society and disciplines of the city of God.[12]

Augustine's writings would inform monasticism in the centuries following the collapse of the Western Empire, and he would be regarded as the primary intellect of the Western world into the Renaissance and beyond.

Boethius

The Latin West in the 5th and 6th centuries witnessed an evaporation of classical knowledge and wisdom, the sources of which were in Greek. The last

---

[12] Fletcher, 30-31.

Roman emperor in the West, Romulus, was deposed in 476 by the German Odoacer. Odoacer left much of the Roman governmental structure in place, including the Senate. Odoacer was overthrown in 493 by Theoderic, King of the Ostragoths. Theoderic had been educated in Greece and was a great admirer of Roman law. Although as an Ostragoth Theoderic was Arian, he maintained harmonious relations with the Catholics.

Anicius Manlius Severinus Boethius (c. 480 – 424 or 426) was born into an aristocratic Roman family of wealth and political power. The family had converted to Christianity at the time of Constantine. When his father died, Boethius was adopted by another influential Roman family and given an extensive education in Greece, becoming expert in both philosophy and theology. He became a Roman senator at age 25 and consul before the age of 30, largely ceremonial positions to be sure as the real power by this time lay with Theodoric in Ravenna. His positions nonetheless indicated that Boethius had achieved all of the prestige and power that could be had in Rome.

Boethius's real accomplishments lay in his intellectual output. He intended to translate into Latin (and provide commentary on) the complete works of Plato and Aristotle. He would not complete this project, but his Latin translations of Aristotle provided an important resource through the Middle Ages. It would be seven centuries before the Greek originals would be rediscovered and become the subject of extensive commentary by Thomas Aquinas.

Theoderic, valuing the skills of the most literary minds, named Boethius as his Master of Offices in court at Ravenna, which made Boethius essentially the gatekeeper to the seat of power. This was no ceremonial position. But in about 523-24, Boethius found himself the victim of political intrigues. He was accused of treason and placed under house arrest pending execution. During this time he wrote his most important work, *The Consolation of Philosophy*. The work combines verse and prose as Lady Wisdom appears to Boethius to diagnose and heal his despondency over all that he had lost. Boethius follows a path similar to that of Augustine to reconcile classical philosophy with Christian faith.

Boethius's writing on Aristotelian logic includes a series of treatises to clarify the four mathematical disciplines of the *quadrivium*, one of which is his *De institutione musica*. In it, Boethius draws on the Pythagorean principles of cosmic harmony existing in a three-fold hierarchy:

- *Musica mundana*, the highest level, is frequently referred to as "music of the spheres." It is the harmony of the universe, the seasons and the harmonious movement of the planets. This is the music heard at the throne of God when the angels sing, "Holy, Holy, Holy, is the Lord of Hosts." This music is heard by God but men lack the sensitivity to hear it.
- *Musica humana* is music of the human body, which includes the harmony between the body and soul.
- *Musica instrumentalis*, the lowest, is music that is actually sounding. It is the audible realization and demonstration of the beauty of numerical ratios.

Boethius writes that music is number made audible, and argues that all beauty can be expressed in terms of numerical ratios. Simpler ratios in music produce more beautiful harmonies. He posits this as all emanating from the perfection of God.

Boethius's *The Consolation of Philosophy* would be widely read and translated throughout the Middle Ages. His philosophical writings in Latin would provide Western Europe with its link to the classical past.

MONASTIC RULES

St. Pachomius (286-346) formed the first community of monks in the Egyptian desert, and is credited with organizing this communal (*cenobitic*) form of monasticism under a set of rules. Monks lived together under the leadership of an abbot and held property in common. This *cenobitic* model thrived alongside the solitary (*eremitic*) model of St. Anthony, spreading west through North Africa and north to Syria. St. Basil the Great (c. 329-379), a bishop in Asia Minor established certain precepts for monastic communities in his *Ascetica* that are still followed today by monks of the Eastern Orthodox Church.

St. John Cassian (c. 360 – c. 435) was likely born in what is today Romania and received a formal education in Latin and Greek. He traveled to Bethlehem, entering a monastic community there, and then on to Egypt. After becoming embroiled in doctrinal controversies in about 399, he left Egypt and sought the protection of St. John Chrysostom in Constantinople. When St. John Chrysostom was forced into exile in 404, Cassian was sent to Rome to argue his case before Pope Innocent I. While there, he was asked to establish an Egyptian-style monastery in Europe near Marseilles.

St. Benedict of Nursia (c. 480 – 543 or 547) was born to a Roman noble. Benedict abandoned his education as a young man and became a hermit, living in a cave in the mountains near Subiaco. He formed 12 communities of monks in that area before establishing the great monastery of Monte Cassino in 530. The Rule of St. Benedict, which follows many of the precepts of John Cassian, governs the spiritual lives of monks and also provides rules for the administration of the monastery.

Monte Cassino was sacked by the Lombards in 580 (See Chapter 7), and the monks fled to Rome, spreading the Benedictine influence. Biographical writings on Benedict are attributed to Pope Gregory the Great, the namesake of Gregorian chant and the pope who sent St. Augustine of Canterbury in 597 to evangelize England (a topic we take up in Unit 7). By the 9th century, the Benedictine rule would be the standard throughout Western Europe.

The Daily Offices

One can find many terms for the daily cycle of prayers observed in monasteries: daily offices, canonical hours, divine office, *opus Dei*, liturgy of the hours, or simply offices. The frequent turning to prayer each day derives from several biblical passages.

"Seven times a day I praise you. . . ." [Psalm 119]

Certain scriptural readings were assigned to each office with a heavy emphasis on psalms. All 150 psalms will ordinarily be sung in a regular recurring cycle every two weeks.

The prayers and scripture readings were of course chanted, and therefore certain chant melodies were assigned to specific offices. Just as the psalms became ingrained in a monk's consciousness through constant repetition, the melodies formed a standard repertoire that would be passed down orally. As techniques developed for notating these melodies, they would be written down in manuscripts.

The Rule of St. Benedict specifies eight offices, or prayers services, that occur each day:

- Matins – the nighttime vigil that would end at dawn
- Lauds – early morning
- Prime – first hour (6 a.m.)

- Terce – third hour (9 a.m.)
- Sext – sixth hour (noon)
- None – ninth hour (3 p.m.)
- Vespers - sunset
- Compline – the final service at the end of the day

These precise rubrics for these offices developed over time and varied somewhat in actual practice, but the regimen of daily prayer and psalm singing became the focus of life within the monastery.

REGIONAL STYLES OF CHANT

We follow primarily the development of the liturgy known as the Roman rite, which became the prevailing practice of the Christian church in Europe. That tradition continues even now in the Roman Catholic Church and in many Protestant denominations. It also has had an indelible influence on all of Western music through today, including secular forms. It was the musical language that Europe learned and from which we can draw clear lines through the flowering of the Renaissance, the classical masterpieces, and into today's popular styles.

But there were, and remain, other styles of chant that developed in other regions of Christendom. In the East, we can classify a variety of chant as Syrian, Coptic (from Egypt and Ethiopia), Persian, and Byzantine. In the West, one would find Roman, Gallican, Sarum, Celtic, Ambrosian, and Mozarabic. One can make a fascinating study of church history—through various conflicts over doctrine and heresies, regional conflicts, and the Muslim conquest—and see how some of these styles were isolated and how others were merged into another tradition. For example, Egypt was taken over early in the Muslim conquest in 641 and was subjected to strong Arabic influences. Celtic chant developed after St. Patrick, who had studied in Gaul, brought Christianity to Ireland. Celtic chant spread into England and Scotland and was later brought back to the European continent by missionaries from Ireland. That tradition was largely absorbed, however, as St. Boniface established monasteries through much of today's Germany to be followed soon by a campaign under Pepin and Charlemagne to standardize the Roman rite throughout Europe. Christians in much of the Iberian Peninsula came under Muslim rule in 711 and remained so for centuries. They would follow the Mozarabic rite, which showed Arabic influences, until the long *Reconquista* succeeded sufficiently to usher in the Roman rite. The Mozarabic rite would be suppressed in 1085.

Byzantium, the eastern half of the Roman Empire, successfully fought Muslim domination until 1453. The Greek and Russian Orthodox Church share a musical tradition that developed largely on its own terms, independent of Rome and Islam. We will take a closer look at this well-established and documented chant of the Eastern Orthodox tradition in Unit 9.

Musicologists face significant challenges in accurately reconstructing the early practices of the Roman and Orthodox churches where we have the most evidence, and those problems are amplified when dealing with some of the other styles that left a more sparse historical record. But one can still find churches that follow many of these traditions and hear chant that has been passed down for centuries. It is a reminder that our best evidence of music often lies in oral tradition.

6. Word and Sacrament

The Abbey of Cluny in France was founded in 910 and flourished from the second half of the 10th century through the early 12th century. We take up this topic now even though it falls outside our chronological progression because it provides a good example of where monasticism would lead. We think it will be helpful for the student to understand the enormous influence and power that the monasteries would accrue.

Cluny was not just another monastery among the thousands of Benedictine monasteries that dotted Western Europe. It was the most famous and the most influential. The first abbey church was consecrated in 915. It was replaced by a much larger structure begun in 954. The third abbey, built between 1088 and 1095, was the largest building in Europe until the 16th century when it was surpassed by the new St. Peter's Basilica in Rome.

2. CLUNY (NO).

Among the factors propelling Cluny to prominence was the stipulation that it remain free of any local authority whether lay or ecclesiastical. It would answer to the pope alone. And it had a strong administration. Benedictine monasteries had always been autonomous communities, but Cluny established a network of monasteries, each headed by a prior (rather than an abbot) who was under the authority of the Abbot of Cluny. The pope extended the privileges enjoyed by Cluny to these subsidiary communities as well, making membership in the Cluny network highly desirable. Cluny monks were not required to do manual labor. The liturgy was their work, and this attracted both monks and benefactors.

Cluny played an important role in the reforms of Pope Gregory VII, which established papal superiority over secular rulers. Its library held one of the largest collections in Europe. It was the jumping off point for pilgrimage routes to Rome and Santiago de Compostela. It participated in the 10th-century Peace of God movement that promoted the safety of noncombatants. With its network of monasteries giving it unprecedented reach and its monks dedicated to the observance of the liturgy, Cluny became a center of arts and culture for all of Europe.

THE BROAD OUTLINES OF THE LITURGICAL YEAR:

Advent: The Church Year begins with the first Sunday of Advent. There are four Sundays in Advent immediately preceding Christmas. Advent ends on Christmas Eve.

Christmas: There are 12 days of Christmas, the first being December 25.

Epiphany begins immediately after Christmas on January 6.

Lent is a 40-day season of fasting that leads up to Easter. It begins on Ash Wednesday.

Holy Week begins with Palm Sunday, the week before Easter. It is a part of Lent.

Easter occurs on the Sunday following the first full moon after the vernal equinox, so it can fall any time within the month following March 21.[13] The season of Easter continues for 40 days until the Ascension.

The **Ascension** always falls on a Thursday, the 40th day after Easter Sunday.

Pentecost occurs on Sunday, the 50th day of Easter or 10 days after the Ascension.

---

[13] The Eastern Christian Church calculates Easter differently, so frequently Orthodox Easter falls on a different date.

Ordinary Time: the remainder of the year may be referred to as the Season after Pentecost. It is measured by how many weeks have elapsed since Pentecost, e.g. the Fifth Sunday after Pentecost or the 18th Week of Pentecost. This continues until the first Sunday of Advent.

THE FIVE PARTS OF THE ORDINARY OF THE MASS:

We have already identified the five parts of the Ordinary of the Mass. Each part plays a role in the overall dramatic shape of worship.

Kyrie eleison. Lord, have mercy. As the worship service begins, the congregant comes in humility and acknowledges his dependence on God's mercy.

Gloria. Glory to God in the Highest. The congregant praises and thanks God for His great mercies.

Credo. I believe in one God. After the scripture readings and sermon, the congregant responds with an affirmation of faith.

Sanctus et Benedictus. Holy, Holy, Holy. The Communion begins with the congregant singing the song sung by the angels Isaiah and Revelation, symbolizing the unison Heaven with redeemed humanity.

Agnus Dei. Lamb of God. Sung at the breaking of the bread to commemorate the sacrifice of Christ that takes away the sins of the world.

THE PROPER OF THE MASS

The Proper of the Mass is comprised of those parts of the liturgy that are specific to the day or the occasion being celebrated. The main parts of the Proper are:

Introit – a fragment of a psalm sung with an antiphon as the celebrant and ministers enter the church and approach the altar.

Gradual or Alleluia – a responsorial psalm sung after the reading of the Epistle by the deacon or other chanter with a response sung by the choir between verses.

Alleluia or Tract – sung before the reading of the Gospel, the Alleluia was a florid chant, which would be replaced in penitential seasons with a more somber chant known as a tract.

Offertory – usually several verses of a psalm sung responsorially by soloists to accompany the procession of the bread and wine to the altar.

Communion – a refrain sung with a psalm during the distribution of the Eucharist.

Getting to Know Manuscripts

As we follow our story of Early Sacred Music, we'll see that more and more manuscripts containing specific information and documentation will survive the ravages of time. The enemies of manuscripts (whether papyrus or parchment) still wrought their damage, though: fire, flood, mold, rodents, fading of ink, and general deterioration. Considering the great enemies of manuscripts, it's amazing *any* of them came down to us!

For our course, we want to get comfortable with some of the terminology used and see how manuscripts were made. We want to know how scholars work with them. It's fascinating forensic work and specialists drawn to this work come from many different backgrounds, bringing an impressive combination of skills to the task.

Psalms from the Dead Sea Scrolls

We need first to consider one of the tectonic changes in the history of writing: the Codex or bound pages in a book. The Codex came into use at about the time of Christ, and Christianity played a key role in promoting its use. Writing before that time had been on scrolls. Scrolls, however, required more surface area because the writing was all on one side. That made them larger and heavier. But there was a more important difference. With a Codex, the reader could access information more easily in a random order, flipping to whatever page he needed to find. In contrast, the scroll was presented in a linear fashion. Many scholars argue that this difference had a profound effect on how people think, but it surely had the effect at least of changing how people digest written information.

The study of manuscripts becomes an important part of music history as we move forward in time.

7. From Barbarians to Charlemagne

We have seen the rise of monasteries after Christianity became the official religion of the Roman Empire under Constantine. And we have examined the Daily Offices and the development of the Mass in the early Middle Ages. But we need to understand something of the political developments of the time because the church history and political history go hand in hand. We will look briefly at Northern Europe (Gaul) under the Merovingian Dynasty, the wars on the Italian peninsula leading to the invasion of the Lombards, and the conversion of England by St. Augustine of Canterbury and the Benedictines.

THE FALL OF ROME AND ITS AFTERMATH

Europe had experienced waves of migration for several centuries. Germanic tribes pushing westward and southward had put increasing strains on Rome's northern border along the Danube. In the late 4th century, Rome was no longer able to hold back the tide, and the invaders entered Roman territory. In 410, Visigoths sacked the city of Rome. The Visigoths moved on to Gaul and from there to the Iberian Peninsula.[14] Barbarians continued to flow into the Western Empire, and in 476 a confederation of tribes under Odoacer deposed the Roman Emperor Romulus Augustulus, marking the official end of Roman rule in the West. Odoacer pledged loyalty to the emperor in Constantinople. But Odoacer in turn was defeated by the Ostragoths under Theodoric in 493. Theodoric "the Great" would rule until 526. In 535, the Roman Emperor Justinian sensed a chance to reconquer the territory of the Western Empire that had been lost. Twenty years of costly war with the Ostragoths significantly weakened both sides and left the Italian Peninsula depopulated. Another Germanic tribe, the Lombards, seized the opportunity and claimed large swaths of Italy.

---

[14] The Visigothic Kingdom would convert to Christianity and flourish in Spain until it was conquered by Muslims in 711-712.

In Gaul, western Germanic tribes known as the Franks had been aligned with Rome in the 5th century. The various tribes would be united by Clovis I, who established the first Frankish dynasty. From Clovis's grandfather, Merovech, they derived the name Merovingian (descendants of Merovech). By his death in 511, Clovis would conquer most of what had been Roman Gaul. In 496, Clovis was baptized into the Catholic faith, which led many of his people to convert as well. Thus Clovis became an ally of the papacy and would be considered the founder of France.

Consider some of the people most prominent in our study and how their lives fit into this historical context at the end of the Western Empire:

- St. Augustine (354-430) would write *City of God* in response to the sacking of Rome in 410.

- Boethius (480-524) would serve in a powerless Roman Senate and then at the real seat of power as right-hand man to Theodoric the Great.

- St. Benedict (480-543 or 547), the same age as Boethius, would found monasteries in Italy during Theodoric's reign and live to see the war between Justinian and the Ostragoths.

- Pope Gregory I (540-604), son of a Roman Senator, would grow up as Justinian fought the Ostragoths and come of age as the Lombards established their kingdom.

ANTIPHON AND PSALMODY

Psalmody is a term often used to describe the singing of psalms in certain Protestant traditions. The Puritans, for example, brought metrical psalmody with them to the American colonies. But psalmody refers more generally to any singing of psalms and has roots far older than any form of Protestantism. Yet there are interesting links. One who wanted to trace the origins of modern Protestant psalmody would find his way back to Gregorian chant and its precursors. That is just one of the ways that the ancient music presented in our study has remained a vital part of worship today.

An antiphon is a Latin chant sung in association with a psalm, typically before and after the psalm. The term *antiphon* has a complex history. It appeared in early Greek writings to signify the interval of an octave. It was sometimes used to describe the alternate signing of male and female choirs (which would naturally produce vocal parts an octave apart). Lady Egeria, who will make a cameo appearance later in this course, used the term to describe a piece sung with a psalm in the liturgy of 4th-century Jerusalem. But the understanding that would have applied in medieval liturgy owes much to St. Ambrose who used the term to describe chants repeated as a refrain after each verse of the psalm. St. Benedict applied the term to a separate chant sung with a psalm.

The texts of antiphons tend to be short and have biblical origins. The antiphon melodies were crafted to make a unified whole with the psalm and to provide a clear cadence on the final note, providing a sense of completion.

Now let us consider a specific antiphon performed in the accompanying video. As you listen to this structure—antiphon / psalm / antiphon—try to hear the specific sections. Also, you will see the chant notation—the written notes, using a system we will call Black Notation. We will learn more about notation soon. This antiphon is taken from an important collection of liturgical texts and melodies called the *Liber Usualis* or, literally, the Usual Book (the book usually used). This collection, a cornerstone of chant practice, contains chants for the Mass and for many texts of the Offices. It was compiled in 1896 by the monks of Solesmes. The singing you will hear is by the monks at Our Lady of Clear Creek, a Benedictine monastery recently established in Oklahoma – the same monastery that we visited in Unit 5 of this course. The monastery has extended many courtesies to us, and we thank them for allowing us to reproduce the recording for this course.

Follow the text as you listen.

Antiphon

Ecce ancilla Domini:
fiat mihi secundum verbum tuum.

Antiphon

Behold the handmaid of the Lord:
be it done unto me according to thy word.

Psalm 126 (Vulgate)

1 canticum graduum Salomonis nisi Dominus aedificaverit domum in vanum laboraverunt qui aedificant eam nisi Dominus custodierit civitatem frustra vigilavit qui custodit

2 vanum est vobis ante lucem surgere surgere postquam sederitis qui manducatis panem doloris cum dederit dilectis suis somnum

Psalm 127 (King James)

1 (A Song of degrees for Solomon.) Except the LORD build the house, they labour in vain that build it: except the LORD keep the city, the watchman waketh but in vain.

2 It is vain for you to rise up early, to sit up late, to eat the bread of sorrows: for so he giveth his beloved sleep.

3 ecce hereditas Domini filii mercis fructus ventris

3 Lo, children are an heritage of the LORD: and the fruit of the womb is his reward.

4 sicut sagittae in manu potentis ita filii excussorum

4 As arrows are in the hand of a mighty man; so are children of the youth.

5 beatus vir qui implebit desiderium suum ex ipsis non confundentur cum loquentur inimicis suis in porta

5 Happy is the man that hath his quiver full of them: they shall not be ashamed, but they shall speak with the enemies in the gate.

Gloria patri

Antiphon

Antiphon

Ecce ancilla Domini:
fiat mihi secundum verbum tuum.

Behold the handmaid of the Lord:
be it done unto me according to thy word.

The *Gloria Patri* (sometimes known as the Lesser Doxology) is typically added after the last verse of the psalm.

CHARLEMAGNE AND ALCUIN OF YORK

Charlemagne set the wheels in motion for significant advances in education and in efforts to recover the intellectual resources of antiquity. Music was not just an incidental beneficiary of this movement. Reading and music-making both were essential to worship and to learning, so it is no surprise that Charlemagne would focus much of his effort on raising the musical standards and finding ways to transmit and preserve musical knowledge. Here we see the beginnings of musical notation, first using a system of neumes to provide a graphic representation of the melody.

While Charlemagne himself was not well educated, he understood its importance and enlisted the best minds he could find, most notably Alcuin of York (735-804). Alcuin received his education at the school founded by Ecgbert, the Archbishop of York and brother of the King of Northumbria. Ecgbert was greatly influenced by Bede the Venerable. The school at York was one of the finest at the time and had a library unequaled in Western Europe. Upon graduation, Alcuin became a teacher at the school and rose to the post of headmaster. He became a deacon and lived as a monk.

When Alcuin was sent to Rome in 781 to carry a petition to the pope, he met Charlemagne and was persuaded to join his entourage of scholars. From 782 to 790 Alcuin resided at the court of Charlemagne where he managed the court school and provided instruction for Charlemagne and his family. But Charlemagne encouraged a much wider reform of education, including an effort to standardize curricula and write textbooks. These would promote the use of a more learned form of Latin to counter its digression into regional dialects. Alcuin is credited with establishing the *trivium* and *quadrivium* as the basis of education.

Alcuin's schools also set up a regimen for teaching music and the singing of chant in the Roman form.

> Charles [Charlemagne] was greatly annoyed by the French mode of singing; for, besides, that their harsh guttural dialect was by no means adapted to melody, the people imagined the beauty of singing to consist in the loudness of the tone, and consequently endeavored to out-scream each other. The reproach of the Italians was not unjust, that the French roared like wild beasts. It was only necessary for Charlemagne to have once heard the Roman church music, to cause him to desire and attempt an improvement in that of his own subjects. The national vanity of the French rendered them unwilling to admit the superiority of the Roman singing, but Charles proved that it was far better, and commanded that it should be adopted. Pope [Adrian I] who willingly seconded all the king's efforts for the reformation of the church, presented him with his two best singers, Theodore and Benedict, one of whom Charles established at Metz and the other at Soissons. There, everyone who desired to teach singing in any of the other schools, or to become a chorister in a church, was now compelled to acquire the Roman method of singing; in consequence of which this art became thenceforth general on this side of the Alps, and as perfect as the discordance of the French voices would permit.[15]

The standardization of music instruction in the Roman Rite would result in a standard repertoire of chant that would become known as Gregorian chant.

---

[15] Frederick Lorenz, *Life of Alcuin* (London: Thomas Hurst, St. Paul's Church-Yard), 57-58 .

8. Elaboration

We have discussed the natural inclination of humans to elaborate on things, to decorate and ornament our surroundings and even ourselves. The very act of creating a work of art flows at least in part from this desire (although a work that merely decorates lacks some essential qualities of art). Of course, we like to make our music more elaborate as well. Modern examples are everywhere; just consider what is done routinely to the National Anthem at sporting events.

THE BEGINNINGS OF POLYPHONY (ORGANUM)

The move from monophony to polyphony in church music can be seen as a natural progression. But as Dr. Christopher Anderson points out in the video, polyphonic music did not come into use because it had suddenly been discovered or invented. Rather a particular style of polyphony, one that was carefully controlled, gained acceptance as appropriate for worship. Monophonic chant had served the purpose of conveying the sacred texts with clarity and solemnity. Polyphonic music would not be admitted into the service unless it reasonably conformed to this aesthetic. (Never mind that it would continue to grow ever more elaborate until church authorities felt a need to rein it in.)

Early organum was characterized by two voices singing the same melody but on different pitches separated by a consonant interval. When one voice ascended or descended in pitch, the other voice did the same. The consonant interval separating the voices was either a perfect fourth or perfect fifth, which, as Pythagoras had taught long ago, were based on the simplest mathematical ratios (perfect fifth = 3:2 and perfect fourth = 4:3).[16] This type of organum was called *parallel* because the added voice moved in parallel motion to the

---

[16] The ratio 2:1 produces the interval of an octave. Music doubled at the octave would still be perceived as monophonic and naturally occurs when women and men sing the same melody.

original chant voice. The earliest written examples are found in the second half of the 9th century in the anonymous treatise *Musica enchiriadis* (Music Handbook). The original chant melody was referred to as the *vox principalis* and the added voice as *vox organalis* (or organal voice).

Another type of early organum involved *oblique* motion where one voice moved and the other stayed on the same pitch. The two voices would begin in unison. As one voice remained static the other would move stepwise until the interval between the two reached a perfect fourth or perfect fifth. The two voices would then likely reverse the process and end in unison. One can also find examples of *free organum* in which the *vox organalis* might mirror the *vox principalis* or cross over it.

All of these styles involved a second voice singing "note for note" with the original. By the end of the 10th century, however, a different form of organum had appeared in which the *vox organalis* was in *melismatic* form, meaning it contained multiple notes per syllable of text and thus more notes than the syllabic *vox principalis* below it. This melismatic organum is often called *florid organum*. It is more elaborate. The original chant melody in the *vox principalis* remained sacrosanct, but the *vox organalis* was freer and had greater expressive possibilities. As the number of notes in the melismatic *vox organalis* increased, the notes in the *vox principalis* had to be held longer. The *vox principalis* or original chant voice came to be known as the *tenor* (Latin *tenere* to hold), and the *vox organalis* as simply *duplum*. We associate this melismatic organum primarily with the Abbey of St. Martial in Limoges. It may also be called "Aquitanian organum" from the region in which Limoges is located.

The preexisting chant melody in the *vox principalis* eventually came to be known as the *cantus firmus* (fixed song). That term appears first in the 14th century, but it describes the same technique that we see in early organum with the use of a chant melody as the basis for a new polyphonic composition. We will take up later developments in organum, particularly the Notre Dame School of the late 12th and early 13th century, in a future unit.

CREATING MANUSCRIPTS

The binding of a manuscript was a critical aspect of its production. To bind means to sew or otherwise rivet the various pages, or folios, together. Pages often were first sewn into groups, called gatherings. So the person doing the binding would be gathering the pages, so to speak, sewing them together, or compressing and gluing them, so as to stabilize them between the cover. The covers could be tooled leather, wood, or metal. Clasps were of metal or leather. Bindings could have decorations of gold, silver, and semi-precious stones.

Bindings often form a kind of biographical identity around a manuscript, and that identity can change over time. An expensive display manuscript designed for presentation would always be given the finest binding, its leather tooled by the finest craftsmen, or its wooden cover decorated by brass clasps with semi-precious stones embedded. But a manuscript designed for daily and hard usage might not be bound at all initially (consider the musical parts copied out for singers or other documents which needed regular consultation). Later it might be bound in practical, durable material, so as to be opened and referred to easily. Over the centuries, bindings would be replaced. Old manuscripts might have their text scraped or washed off so that the parchment could be reused. Or, manuscripts might be seen as more valuable as time passed, and a practical, daily-use manuscript might be viewed as historically important and rebound more elegantly.

With rebinding, though, sometimes the pages of a manuscript (which would fray with use) would be cut or trimmed down to become even or to fit within a slightly smaller binding. In the process, valuable information might be cut off, including dating, words of text or notes of music, and names that would reveal something about the persons or place where the manuscript had its origin. Marginalia (a topic we discuss below) could be lost.

Provenance

Following the origin and path of a manuscript can also be fascinating. There's a term for it: provenance or provenience. It means all the places the manuscript has been and people to whom it has belonged. Implicit are also the purposes for which it has been used. Provenance is a natural part of how we view things, if you think about it. Almost everyone has some object that belonged to a relative several generations ago. Perhaps it's an old teddy bear, which the little child is told belonged to great uncle Rudolph but then was given to Great Grandma when she settled in the heartland of Kansas. And from there, Teddy went with the next generation of children to San Francisco. And so the story goes, until it ends up in this child's hands. That's the path or story of the Teddy Bear. Provenance is the path or story of the manuscript.

More interesting, although not as impressive or beautiful, were the practical, functional manuscripts, which were created to be used by singers, conductors, or instrumentalists. They rarely employed color, unless the colors were functional. Elaborations in the copyists' hand would be few.

Inks

What is ink, after all, but stain that leaves its color on a surface? And the stains that were used were varied and fascinating. Soot, pounded and soaked barks, plant leachings, nut stains, ferrous sulfate, burnt bones, tar and pitch, crushed minerals, and wine were among the ingredients used for making ink.

Parchment

Of course, none of the issues we've discussed, from content to layout, from illuminations to binding, would exist without consideration of the basic issue: the material upon which the manuscript was written, the parchment.

Parchment is a general term for animal skin. Parchment replaced papyrus, clay, and stone as the preferred material for writing upon by the 4th century. Parchment took many different forms. There were fine vellums (calf skin) and skins from sheep and goats. There were infinite gradations of animal skins and, as you might expect, production of parchment became a huge business. This stayed true until it was replaced by paper in the late Renaissance. Yet, even once the spread of printing presses pushed production to the point that the new improved papers were the best choice for books, parchment was still used for printing and even is used today in special situations.

The process for making parchment is simple, but time consuming. Skins are soaked, treated with lime, scraped, and then stretched to dry. They are not tanned, which means they are not as durable as leather. Parchment was highly developed by the Greeks already in the 3rd century B.C., but its use goes back much further to the ancient Egyptians.

Papyrus, the paper made from pulp and preferred for use in ancient scrolls, had became increasingly expensive in the first centuries of the Christian era, in part because of over harvesting of the reeds. So parchment began to fill the gap.

Unlike papyrus, which could be made in any length or pieced together and rolled into scrolls, parchment had a circumscribed area corresponding to the animal's skin at the widest points. From that limitation, or advantage, depending on how you look at it, a new format sprang forth: the page, or folio to use the Latin. Folio comes from the same root as foliage or leaf. And from these folios, sheets sewn together into groupings called quires and bound together, books were created. The new term used initially, though, was not book, but codex.

NEUMES

We use the word "music" in English to refer to the musical sounds that we hear and also to the musical notation that we see. Someone who is not a musician can be forgiven for thinking they are essentially the same thing. But they are not—no more than a blueprint is building. The notation written or printed on a page, like a blueprint, is just a set of symbols that must be interpreted and then realized. Modern notation has developed to provide reasonably good information, but it is still just a basic outline. The performer must have knowledge of musical styles and practices to turn a page of notes into the right sounds.

Neumes were an early precursor to our system of musical notation and show up in the 9th century. These squiggles on the page gave rather limited and subjective clues concerning pitch in visual form. But whereas some who knew a melody could be reminded of it by these neumes, someone who did not already know the melody would be unlikely to reproduce it accurately from neumes alone. Neumes could indicate shape or contour or direction, but gave no objective information about specific pitches.

Heightened neumes offered a significant advance in the 11th century: each neume was placed vertically to indicate its pitch in relation to the other neumes. In this way it could show the overall pitch contour of the whole piece, not just individual motives and small note groupings. But it still lacked a clear indication of specific pitches. It also took up much more vertical space on the page, which made the manuscripts more expensive.

Objective information concerning pitch would soon be added in the form of a horizontal line. That line would represent a specific pitch (identified by a clef sign), and the neumes could then be placed vertically in relation to that line. With this feature, the beginnings of the musical staff had arrived, an improvement generally attributed to the Italian music theorist Guido of Arezzo (d. 1033). Greater clarity could be achieved by adding additional lines to represent adjacent pitches. Standardization would take some time, but the concept of the modern musical staff was in place.

INTRODUCTION TO THE ECCLESIASTICAL MODES

Although the terminology is similar, the system for designating the ecclesiastical or church modes in the Middle Ages differs from the ancient Greek modes. So a reference to "Dorian," for example, in Plato's writings does not mean the Dorian mode as understood in Western music. Students of this course do not need to identify or fully understand the modes, but those with some musical training may want to explore them.

One can understand the modes generally as similar to the major and minor scales, but with different arrangements of whole and half steps. Using the white keys on the piano and playing the notes from C to the octave above produces a major scale with whole steps and half steps in this order: W W H W W W H. The Dorian mode can be produced in the same way by starting on D, the Phrygian starting on E, the Lydian starting on F, and the Mixolydian starting on G. In each case, the occurrence of the whole and half steps shifts to different scale degrees.

The tonal system of major and minor is not determined simply by the content of the scale, however, but by the hierarchy of pitches within the scale. There is a tonal center (tonic, or the first scale degree) that predominates. Second in importance is the dominant or fifth scale degree, and the other scale degrees are of subsidiary importance. Modality depends on the same kind of hierarchy. There is a "final" tone more or less equivalent to tonic and a dominant or "reciting tone." The ear distinguishes major and minor by identifying the tonal center and hearing the pitch content of the scale in the context of that tonal center. So just as major and minor have a different character, each or the modes has a character of its own.

The modes remained a prominent feature of Western music throughout the Renaissance until approximately 1600 when the modern tonal system of just two modes (major and minor) began to predominate. But some features of modal music can be found to the end of the baroque period in the music of J.S. Bach, and many 20th-century composers returned to modal forms.

THE FIRST MILLENNIUM

Before turning to Eastern Orthodoxy in the next unit and later developments in polyphony thereafter, it is worth considering Richard Fletcher's summary of the first millennium.

By the year 1000 Christian communities had been planted from Greenland to China. The acceptance of Christianity by these outsiders was not simply a matter of confessional change, of dogma, of religious belief and observance in a narrow sense. It involved, or brought in its wake, a much wider process of change. The conversion of "barbarian" Europe to Christianity brought Roman and Mediterranean customs and values and habits of thought to the newcomers who were the legatees of the Roman empire. These included, for example, literacy and books and the Latin language with all that it opened up; Roman notions about law, authority, property and government; the habits of living in towns and using coin for exchange; Mediterranean tastes in food, drink and costume; new architectural and artistic conventions. The Germanic successor-states which emerged from the wreckage of the empire . . . accepted Christianity and in so doing embraced a cultural totality which was Romanitas, "Roman-ness". It was particularly significant that this occurred at a time when two other processes were shattering the cultural unity of the Mediterranean world. One of these was the withdrawal into herself of the eastern, Byzantine, Orthodox half of the former Roman Empire. The other was the irruption of Islam into the Mediterranean and the resultant hiving off of its eastern and southern shores into an alien culture. The cultural unity of the Mediterranean disappeared forever. But what had been harvested from the classical world and transplanted with Christianity into a northern seedbed germinated there, sprouted and grew into a new civilization, one which indeed owed much to the Mediterranean but was distinctively its own: western European Christendom. The growth of Christendom decisively affected the character of European culture and thereby, because of European dominance in human affairs for several centuries before the twentieth, the civilization of our world.[17]

---

[17] Fletcher, 1-2.

9. Eastern Orthodoxy

The topic of Eastern Christianity invites us to experience new sounds and liturgical practices while considering a non-Western approach to Christian belief. We start by remembering that the Christian world was more or less united for its first millennium. There was, simply put, "Christianity"—with significant regional differences, of course, but one Christian Church dating back to the time of Jesus.

EAST IS EAST

The split between the Eastern and Western branches (centered in Constantinople and Rome) is dated officially as 1054, but many smaller disagreements led up to it. A principal area of disagreement involves the wording of a part of the *Nicene Creed* known as the *filioque*. But keep in mind that the two spheres of Christianity are united by far more than what divides them. Pope John Paul II (1920-2005) worded it beautifully when he urged that "the Church must breathe with her two lungs." (*Et unum sint*, "That they may be one," Encyclical, 1995)

In the video for this unit, you hear Eastern Orthodoxy described as a "spiritually rigorous, yet sensually rich, approach to worship." We are concerned in this course with the aspects of beauty that enrich Orthodoxy—chant, icons, ceremonial grandeur—as well as points of doctrine and differing historical perspectives. The Eastern perspective is explained in part by the fact that the three specific historical movements that shaped Western thought in the second millennium did not affect the Orthodox Church, namely the Reformation, the Enlightenment, and the artistic reaction to the Enlightenment known as Romanticism. This fact alone explains why the "two lungs" have diverged even more since the schism in 1054.

As in Western Christianity, Orthodox music, architecture, and icons serve as earthly symbols of a Divine Reality. In the Eastern tradition, though, these elements are fixed, accepted, and not open to debate, reform, or reconstitution. They are to be expressed consistently. While this consistency may seem inflexible or limiting to the Western mind, it is a testament to the absolute doctrines of faith that characterize Eastern Christian worship.

BYZANTIUM

The spiritual and logistical home of Eastern Orthodoxy was Byzantium, a city first colonized by the Greeks in 657 B.C. Located at the only entrance to the Black Sea, it became a significant center of trade and culture. Its Christian identity resulted from the presence of Constantine the Great (272-337) who had embraced the religion. His mother Helena (250-330) had been baptized decades earlier.

Constantine oversaw critical events in early Christian history, including the Council of Nicea in 325 and the founding of the Church of the Holy Sepulcher in Jerusalem. Byzantium was renamed Constantinople in 333, and today Constantine and Helena are celebrated as major saints throughout the Christian world.

After the Western Empire "fell" in 476, Byzantium became Christendom's primary center and began to be known as the "New Rome." Ottoman Turks under Mehmed II conquered the city of Constantinople in 1453. The magnificent Holy Cathedral of Hagia Sophia (Holy Sophia) was converted into a mosque—a drastic action that even today saddens the Christian world. Still the name Constantinople lasted until the early 20th century (1929), when the city was given the Arabic name Istanbul.

Until its fall to Islam in 1453, Constantinople remained Eastern Christendom's geographic and spiritual home. From its beginnings, the practice of Eastern Christianity was shaped by the Greek language and Greek aesthetics. Orthodoxy proudly links its spiritual heritage back to its classical origins.

THE SPREAD OF ORTHODOXY

Beginning in the 9th century, the Byzantine Christians launched a vital, far-reaching missionary effort. The most famous of all Greek missionaries from this period were two brothers known throughout Christianity as St. Cyril and St. Methodius. Cyril and Methodius were born into an upper-class family in Thessalonika. After stellar achievements in education, linguistics, even politics, they both renounced the world and became monks. They were sent on multiple missions to convert, first, the Khazars in the Dnieper-Volga region and then the Moravians. Their missionary zeal spread through the Southern Slavic lands. They developed a new alphabet to translate the scriptures (Glagolitic) and are credited, by tradition, with extending a rudimentary alphabet developed by Bulgarians and laying the basis for the liturgical language still used today by Orthodox Slavs (Old Church Slavonic).

Their insistence on cultivating the Slavonic language (the vernacular) for saying Mass was a bold decision that continues to be honored today. Often in iconography the brothers are depicted as an Eastern bishop and a monk, one holding up the translated Bible or a model of a church, and the other a scroll with Old Church Slavonic letters.

THE BAPTISM OF RUSSIA

The Conversion of Russia to Eastern Christianity began in what today is Kiev in the year 988 with the baptism of Prince Vladimir I (c. 945-c. 1015). His own grandmother had converted to Christianity in 950. Again, a mother (in this case, grandmother) led the way!

Prince Vladimir's conversion was as much a political event as a religious one. He not only was forging alliances for military campaigns, but he also understood the need to adopt to a national religion to unify and strengthen his nascent kingdom, particularly in light of the internecine struggles that had destabilized princedoms in early *Rus*. Until these early Slavonic princes developed a system of primogeniture where the eldest son inherited the rule, there could be no political stability.

According to a famous legend in Russia's earliest preserved historical document known as *The Primary Chronicles*, Vladimir sent emissaries far away to experience the world's religions. They were dismayed by the dietary and alcohol restrictions of Islam, and unimpressed by the Diaspora of the Jews, who had been expelled from Israel in Old Testament times and were still without a homeland (not a good model for building a strong nation-state). Adopting Western Christianity as practiced in Rome presented problems as well: an allegiance to the pope would be required, and that was seen as an outside threat to national unity.

But the emissaries' encounter with Eastern Christianity dazzled them. The beauty of the singing, the incense, the icons, and the fact that the church's hierarchy consisted of equally authoritative local patriarchs appealed to them. So they returned to Vladimir with the suggestion that his new nation be baptized as Eastern Orthodox. Or so the legend goes.

This legend endures powerfully within Slavic culture, as it lays out principles and conventions operative today in Russian culture (rejection of outside influence, love of visual and aural beauty, cultural indulgences in alcohol and diet). It needs also to be strongly emphasized that all of these historical events took place in and around today's Kiev, making the real birthplace of Russian Christianity the region known today as Ukraine.

THE ORTHODOX LITURGY

Eastern Christians have employed various forms of the Greek word *Liturgia* to describe the central act of worship that culminates in the celebration of the Eucharist or Communion. In the Western tradition, the term *Mass* is used, derived from the Latin *Missa*. In both Eastern and Western traditions, the readings and prayers in these services have been largely chanted (sung) as far back as the written record can document, and both initially were sung *a cappella* or voices only. But over time, the chanting of the Western Mass began to be supported by instruments, primarily the organ. After the Middle Ages a strong and far-reaching tradition of instrumental accompaniment and independent instrumental pieces developed in Western Christianity.

This development did not occur within Eastern Christianity. The Orthodox *Liturgia* was (and still is) chanted without accompaniment of any kind of instrument (*a cappella*) with very few exceptions. For example, some Greek parishes established in the United States installed organs to play sparse instrumental support for the chanting, but this was considered to be part of a desire to assimilate to the New World.

STRUCTURE OF THE ORTHODOX LITURGY

Both Eastern *Liturgia* and Western Mass share common structures and many identical texts. But some elements in the Eastern celebration of the Eucharist differ from Western practice.

One particularly noteworthy difference has been featured in the video: the *Cherubikon* or *Cherubic Hymn*.

Greek Transcribed	English	Old Church Slavonic
I ta cherubin mysticos Iconizontes	We who mystically represent the Cherubim,	Иже херувимы тайно образующе,
ke ti zopion triadi ton trisagyon ymnon prophagentes	and who sing to the Life-Giving Trinity the thrice-holy hymn,	и Животворящей Троицѣ трисвятую пѣснь припѣвающе,
passa nin biotikin apothometa merinnan·	let us now lay aside all earthly cares	Всякое нынѣ житейское отложимъ попеченіе.
Os ton basileon ton olon Ipodoxomeni	that we may receive the King of all,	Яко да Царя всѣхъ подъимемъ,
tes angelikes aoraton doriforumenon taxasin	escorted invisibly by the angelic orders.	ангельскими невидимо дориносима чинми.
alleluia	Alleluia	*Аллилуіа*

Many people find this text, and the liturgical actions that occur during its recitation to be one of the most beautiful parts of the Orthodox Liturgy. The text is sung while the elements of the Eucharist (bread and wine) are brought out from what is called the Table of Oblation behind the Iconostasis through the North Deacon's door, carried through the congregation, and brought back to the Altar through the Holy Doors (middle doors). While Cherubim are biblical and referred to many times in Western Christianity, a parallel text extolling the Cherubim at this critical point in the Eucharistic progression will not be found in the Western Mass.

Here is a good place to mention that there are three sets of texts used for celebrating the Orthodox *Liturgia*. By far the most common is the *Liturgy of St. John Chyrsostom*, attributed to St. John Chrysostom (St. John of the Golden Mouth, c. 349-407). It is sung nearly at every Divine Liturgy.

The remaining two liturgies are employed at specific times during the year: the *Liturgy of St. Basil the Great* is used ten times, including the five Sundays of Lent, the Thursday and Saturday of Holy Week, Christmas Eve, the eve before Epiphany (Theophany), and on the feast day of St. Basil (January 1 of the Orthodox, or Julian, Calendar). The *Liturgy of the Pre-Sanctified Gifts* is used only when the Eucharistic elements have undergone transubstantiation during a previous liturgy (the change from bread and wine to the Body and

Blood of Our Lord). Thus, the elements are "pre-sanctified." This text is sung on Wednesdays and Fridays of Lent, on Thursday of the fifth week of Lent, and the first three days of Passion Week.

STRUCTURE OF THE LITURGY OF ST. JOHN CHRYSOSTOM

The *Liturgy of St. John Chrysostom* is divided into four parts:

1. The Liturgy of Preparation (preliminary steps in preparing the Bread and the Wine that occur behind the Iconostasis)

2. The Liturgy of the Catechumens (focused on psalms, prayers, responses, the Epistle and Gospel reading, as well as the sermon, and open to all of those who are in the beginning stages of becoming Christian)

3. The Liturgy for the Faithful (final preparation of the Communion elements and the Creed, only for baptized Christians)

4. The Eucharistic Canon (the reverent reception of the actual the Communion elements, administered as a mixture of bread and wine)

The entire text of this liturgy in Greek, English, Russian, and many other languages can be found in many places, including on Orthodox websites. Of course, elements such as the prayers and the psalms (highly emphasized in the Liturgy of the Catechumens) do change with the seasons of the church year. But, as in the Ordinary of the Mass, large parts of the text are constant, regardless of the liturgical season.

Also, as in any religious practice, one finds regional inflections. Within Orthodoxy, these alterations are minimal and tend to reflect the circumstances influencing the local parishes or national churches. One historic example was a short but vigorous text sung in Russian Orthodox Churches near the end of the Liturgy during Tsarist times. It translates as "Many Years" (*Mnogaia leta*), and it gave a brief exhortation wishing the tsar "many years" to lead the nation, preserve Orthodoxy, and protect the people. This text, not surprisingly, was set to elaborate music by Russian composers, particularly in the 18th and 19th centuries.

All of this detail reminds us how tightly and intricately organized the traditions of Orthodox worship are, no matter in which country of the world it takes place. A complete study of Orthodoxy liturgy is a massive undertaking, and yet one that is fully engaging and indescribably rewarding.

ART TRADITION *VERSUS* PARISH LITURGICAL PRACTICE

Many people first experience Orthodoxy through hearing a late 19th-century setting of liturgical texts by a romantic-era composer like Sergei Rachmaninov, Alexander Grechaninov, or Pavel Chesnokov. These may be heard on recordings or in concert, and generally leave the listener gloriously overwhelmed by the masses of soaring *a cappella* harmonies. This exceptionally beautiful repertoire has drawn people to a study of Orthodox music, or, indeed, even to the practice of Eastern Orthodoxy.

Yet this specific body of repertoire grew out of a particular historical era of musical "renewal," when composers across both Western and Eastern Europe cast off musical styles based on 17th- and 18th-century Italian classical structures or early 19th-century opera, and returned to their religious roots. Western Catholic composers looked back to Gregorian chant as a basis for their new compositions. Protestant composers rediscovered the rich body of renaissance chorales that had inspired the Reformation. And Russian composers took up the same call for the Orthodox repertoire. An important group of composers wove lines of ancient monophonic chant (*znamenny*) into an extremely rich fabric of late romantic harmonies that spoke to the Slavic ear. The most famous of such composers was Rachmaninov, but there were many more. These composers wrote their works not for a simple (typical) village parish choir of three to six singers, but for the highly trained, large choirs one would find in major cathedrals or conservatories.

Thus, when listening to these works, keep in mind that they were designed for highly capable or professional choirs. The average, small parish choir would not have the vocal resources or musical training to sing such pieces during the celebration of the Liturgy or Offices. Then, as now, the choices of musical settings in the parish practice remains relatively simple, based on familiar chant patterns chosen according to the strict, and ancient rules of "tones" appropriate to the text, the service, and the identity of each day within the liturgical cycle.

Znamenny Notation

Znamenny is an ancient form of single melody Orthodox chant. It is similar in many ways to its sister repertoire in Western Christendom known as Gregorian chant. When first written down, *znamenny* was configured in "staffless" notation based on the use of symbols. From the word for "sign" (*znak*) rose the term *znamenny*. In this kind of notation, words are written down and symbols that indicate the rise and fall of pitches are placed above the words. Rhythm is dictated by the flow of the text. The same development happened in the West with neumes in the earliest Gregorian chant.

Before *znamenny*, the ancient Greeks had also developed an earlier form of sign-notation. It boasted an even more complex set of musical patterns and is known to us today as *Kondakarion* notation.

If both the West and the East began notating chant using words and "signs," then what is different here? In the East, the system of symbols prevailed for centuries longer than in the West. The use of "lines and spaces" (staff notation) was not necessary for writing down *znamenny* chant. The specific intricacies of *znamenny* were conveyed through the exactitude of oral transmission.

Then, in the late 17th and 18th centuries, Western musical influence invaded the Orthodox world, particularly in tsarist Russia. The patterns, intonation, and flexibility of *znamenny* singing would be washed away by the entry of Western staff notation, which, by then, was highly sophisticated. What we today call renaissance and baroque style swept into the Slavonic liturgy, imported consciously because it was perceived as being more sophisticated than the ancient *znamenny* singing. Tsars Alexei I and his son Peter the Great sought to make Russia as Western as they dared. And modernizing the church music was part of the formula. Thus, Western polyphonic style dropped into Orthodox practice fully formed. Imagine a musical earthquake and you have the right idea!

Yet Russian (and Ukranian) composers were attracted to the new musical possibilities of setting significant liturgical texts in Western style. The new compositions were metered (duple or triple beats per measure) and boasted Western-style polyphonic vocal lines and harmonies. This music was written using Western staff notation.

The singing remained *a cappella*, and *znamenny* was retained for chanting prayers and recitations. But the principal texts (like the *Cherubic*

Hymn) began to be set in Western style. Because of the requirements of *a cappella* singing, and the high level of skill brought to the task, Russian sacred singing developed its exceptionally rich sound. It would not be until the end of the 19th century that composers began to rethink some of these outside influences and sought to inject their new sacred works with the purity and power of *znamenny* chant.

As noted in the video, one sector of Russian Orthodoxy never did adopt the new Western-style notation or musical style. They are known as the Old Believers who split from the larger body of Orthodox over controversial doctrinal reforms in the 17th century. The Old Believers have been frequently persecuted since that time. Their continued use of monophonic *znamenny* chant across the centuries is one of many things attesting to their fidelity to (what they perceive as) the true principles of Orthodoxy.

ORTHODOX ARCHITECTURE

The architecture of the early Greek Christian churches set the pattern for Orthodox churches around the world. Virtually every architectural feature in the early Greek churches has consistent theological and liturgical significance and, thus, was *ortho*—true, right, correct, and not open to alteration. The most prominent features are as follows:

External

- Placement of the building. Oriented to the East so that the altar faces east.

- Domes (as opposed to steeples). The number of domes symbolizes something specific. Three = the Trinity; four = the Four Evangelists; two = the Divine and Human nature of Christ, etc.

- Rounded windows with clear, rather than stained glass. Round surfaces symbolize eternity and the vault of heaven; clear glass lets in the unadulterated, pure light of the sun, given us by God.

- Separate Bell Tower (where practical). Bells give important signals concerning the times and meaning of worship services about to take place. Bells "announce" (slow, rhythmic striking), "peal" (ringing within pre-set rhythmic patterns), and sound in what is called "chain-ringing" (beginning with the lowest bell and activating every bell to the highest pitch). Bells also can toll (slow striking of each bell, with all bells sounding at the beginning and end). For Orthodox believers, these patterns convey much specific information across long distances.

Internal

- Iconostasis (Icon Wall). Separates the nave from the altar area, with specific positioning for each type of icon; often in tiers expressing a hierarchy of the images depicted.

- Bema (raised platform at the eastern end on which the altar is placed). Dating back to the practice of law in the pubic forum, the bema is intersected by the iconostasis

- Icons (two-dimensional images, generally in Byzantine style). Icons are windows through which the worshiper encounters the qualities of God, Christ, the Holy Spirit, Holy Mary, the apostles, the prophets and patriarchs, and the saints.

- No Statuary. Three-dimensional imagery evokes the issue of idolatry.

- Candles (best if pure beeswax). Placed in front of the icons for expressing prayers and veneration. Provide a simple, accessible way to glorify God, dispel the darkness, manifest the joy we feel in our souls, bestow honor to the saints and early Christians, inspire good works, ask for forgiveness of our sins.

- Icon of the Last Judgment (on the back, or western, wall). A reminder of human mortality and dependency on God's Grace as the worshiper leaves the consecrated space of the church.

Both the building *and* the grounds of an Orthodox Church are consecrated, and thus are considered holy spaces. Wherever the worshiper stands, he or she actually is *in* the presence of God. If the property or building is desecrated in any way (as Orthodox churches were across Eastern Europe during Communism), it must be reconsecrated by means of a special liturgy. What this means, in terms of worship, is that believers are actually *in* the presence of God, participating in God's sense of time and place. The figures from the past shown in icons (apostles, patriarchs) are actually present and participating in the prayers and supplications. There is, or should be, a suspension of the earthly sense of things, and a complete embrace of God's kingdom.

To the degree that this sense of sacred place and other-worldly time is understood, the nature of everything that happens within the Orthodox services reflects Heaven's realities (or that would be the ideal to which a believer would subscribe). The mystery that attracts many people to the Orthodoxy stems from this embrace of a non-Western view of time and place.

10. Polyphony, Pilgrimage and Crusade

We began in Unit 8 to look at new forms of polyphonic music, in particular the music written by Léonin and Pérotin at Notre Dame in Paris. We refer to this frequently as "the Notre Dame School." In this unit we look more closely at polyphonic music that predates Léonin and Pérotin beginning with Hildegard von Bingen and moving to the organum at St. Martial of Limoges.

EXPANDING POLYPHONY IN AN AGE OF PILGRIMAGE

We need to consider the obvious question of why music became polyphonic. Don't expect this lesson to give you a simple, satisfactory answer. But we can pretty safely rule out two answers that might initially seem logical. First, as we have seen, it was not simply because people suddenly discovered a more sophisticated sound to replace the "primitive" monophonic music. The idea of multiple voices sounding simultaneously was surely around from the earliest of times. Second, it was not a matter of the "conservative" church deciding to catch up with freer secular styles. In fact, it was sacred music that led the way in developing polyphony, and the secular styles that had to play catch-up.

The answer lies more in the development of written notation. With notation came the ability to capture musical ideas on paper and to teach them across time and distance. This ability obviously served the goals of preserving music and standardizing it across a wider geographical territory, addressing the main shortcomings of oral transmission. Notation also facilitated the creation of more elaborate and complex forms of music. It allowed musicians to visualize and better understand the interaction of multiple parts. This put composers in control and allowed them to build even more complex musical structures, just as mathematicians work out complex equations on paper and understand complex equations by viewing them on paper.

The learning necessary to use the tools of notation still resided almost exclusively in the Church. So it should not surprise us that sacred music was able to leap ahead of secular forms in terms of complexity and sophistication. But Europe was becoming less feudal and more prosperous. Cathedral schools and universities were overtaking monasteries as cultural centers. In due time composers would take the skills learned in sacred music and increasingly apply them in the secular world.

PILGRIMAGES

After the fall of Jerusalem, Christians naturally focused on the New Testament promise that God is present everywhere. But in the 4th century, Constantine restored the holy sites and built churches that facilitated worship in those places. Jerusalem became and remained the most important pilgrimage destination for Christians. After the 7th-century Muslim Conquest, Christians continued to travel to Jerusalem and worship in the holy sites. The First Crusade at the end of the 10th century was a response not so much to longstanding Muslim domination of Jerusalem, but to the specific acts that made pilgrimage impossible.

Jerusalem is a long way from Western Europe. European Christians could more easily undertake a journey to Rome or Canterbury. Numerous other sites housing the relics of saints could be found throughout Europe and became popular pilgrimage destinations. Roads were built, and the trek was made easier by monasteries and others catering to the needs of travelers. The pilgrimage trade was big business.

Cluny became one of the most important starting points for pilgrims on the Way to Saint James—Santiago de Compostela in northwestern Spain, where the bones of James the Apostle were said to be buried. Limoges, the home of St. Martial organum, had been absorbed into the Cluniac network in 1063. It was not so much a pilgrimage destination as it was an important way station.

KNIGHTS, CASTLES, AND CHIVALRY

A knight was, by most definitions, simply a warrior with a horse. Horses gave an army mobility and allowed the projection of power over greater distances. Mounted soldiers were not new. Charlemagne made effective use of this mobility, ranging great distances in his many conquests.

With the collapse of the Carolingian Empire and the rise of the Viking raiders, defense became more localized. Castles were built all across Europe in the 9th and 10th centuries for defense. But castles had an offensive purpose as well. They provided a safe haven and base for raids on the countryside and against neighboring fiefdoms. When fiefdoms came into conflict, the way to punish your opponent was to slaughter his peasants and burn his fields. Knights performed such tasks in the service of the local castellan, the owner of the castle, and they answered to no one else. Knights of the 10th century were not likely to think in terms of honor and chivalry. Nor were those who encountered knights likely to expect such things.

The church sought to curb the reckless and violent behavior of knights. At about the time of the first millennium, relics were put to use in an attempt to bring some degree of peace and safety to medieval life. Large outdoor events were held at which the abbots of the monasteries and bishops would assemble as many relics as possible and invite the nobles and knights to attend. Called the "Peace of God" and the "Truce of God," the nobles and their knights were implored to swear off violence. So many relics were bound to leave an impression and prompt the knights to consider what consequences their actions might have in the afterlife. These events, it appears, had rather limited success.

But a Crusade! That had purpose. It was war fought for a cause, not just for plunder and territory. And Pope Urban II apparently saw this as a means of bringing the knights into the service of a higher cause. The First Crusade saw the founding of orders of knights – Knights Hospitalier and Knights of the Holy Sepulcher. Knights Templar followed. The Crusades were thus a significant contributor to the ethos of chivalry.

The concept of chivalry was captured, and maybe even to a significant extent invented, in the literary device of courtly love. And courtly love was made popular and spread through the songs of the Troubadours. It was a literary device. It added an aura of nobility to the knights' service in the Crusades and applied that ideal to knights at home as well. Now courtly love sounds like a wonderfully medieval and long-lost phenomenon, but C.S. Lewis argues that it never went away, at least not as of 1937 when he wrote *An Allegory of Love*. Lewis says

> French poets, in the eleventh century, discovered or invented, or were the first to express, that romantic species of passion which English poets were still writing about in the nineteenth. They

effected a change which has left no corner of our ethics, our imagination, or our daily life untouched, and they erected impassable barriers between us and the classical past or the Oriental present. Compared with this revolution the Renaissance is a mere ripple on the surface of literature.[18]

While this was a secular literary movement, it played a significant role in the arts – as Lewis argues, right up to the present. Without question, it serves for us as a defining feature of the Middle Ages. Therefore, it is worth considering it in this study of sacred music of that time. As we will see, sacred and secular music influenced one another, and some of the ethos and style of Troubadour songs worked its way into certain sacred forms and carried over into the Renaissance.

SPAIN AND THE RECONQUISTA

We have followed sacred Christian music as it moved from Jerusalem into Greece and Rome, to the Frankish Kingdom, England, and across the Holy Roman Empire. The Iberian Peninsula (Spain and Portugal) was Christianized by Visigoths in the 5th century. But music there followed a different path from the rest of Europe because for much of the Middle Ages it was Islamic. The term *Reconquista* (reconquest) refers to the long struggle to restore Christian rule, a process that would span 770 years.

After conquering all of North Africa in the 7th century, Muslims crossed the Mediterranean into the Iberian Peninsula in 711. This force comprised of Arabs and recently converted North African Berbers advanced rapidly against small warring factions of Christian Visogoths, taking all of the Iberian Peninsula and crossing the Pyrenees into France by 714. The Islamic emirate of Al-Andalus was established.

A remnant of Christian resistance remained in northern Spain. In 722, when a Muslim expedition was sent to crush a minor Christian rebellion, the small Christian force defeated the Muslims at the Battle of Covadonga, marking the beginning of the *Reconquista*. Christians would have a foothold in northern Spain from that time forward. The Muslim push into France was ultimately halted by Charles Martel at the Battle of Tours in 732. Islamic rule would be confined the Iberian territory south of the Pyrenees, but this

---

[18] C.S. Lewis, *The Allegory of Love* (Oxford Univ. Press, 1936), 4.

included most of today's Spain and Portugal. Christians in the north of Spain would remain for many years disorganized and subject to shifting alliances, sometimes warring with the Muslims, sometimes with each other, and sometimes allied with the Muslims against other Christians.

The vast Islamic world was controlled by the Umayyad caliphate in Damascus until it was overthrown by the Abbasid Revolution in 750. The Abbasid Dynasty would rule the Muslim Empire until 1285 from its new capital of Baghdad. Virtually all of the Umayyad family were killed in revolution with the exception of Abd al-Rahman, who escaped the slaughter and made his way to Spain. In 756 he unified the Muslims and established the Umayyad Dynasty in Spain. In 929, they began to refer to themselves as a caliphate. They reached their peak of power under Almonzor, but upon his death in 1002, no Muslim successor was able to maintain Muslim unity, and the Umayyad caliphate collapsed in 1031. From that point, the Muslims were weakened by factions and internal strife while the Christians managed to unite and push south.

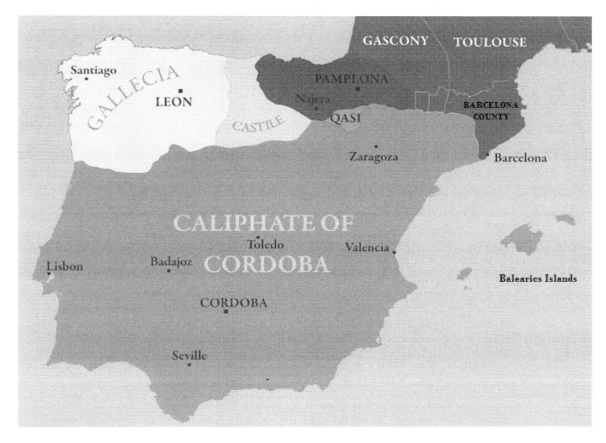

Al-Andalus and Christian Kingdoms c. 1000

In 840, the Christians discovered the bones of St. James in northern Spain. The site attracted pilgrims, and a settlement formed that was called Compostela. The site gained regional political importance, and by the mid 11th century it had become one of the primary pilgrimage sites, second only to Rome and Jerusalem. With attention focused on this pilgrimage site, King Alfonso VI of Castille (c. 1040-1109) was able to rally the Christians and impress on the rest of Europe the importance of the recapturing Spanish territory. The *Reconquista* made critical headway when Alfonso conquered the important city of Toledo and pushed the Muslims into the southern half of the Iberian Peninsula. When the crusading ideology caught fire at the end of the 11th century, most Europeans knights set out for Jerusalem, but the Spanish were not allowed by Pope Urban II to join that crusade. The Spanish had their own crusade to fight at home. That struggle would continue, with each side having the upper hand at times, until 1212 when the Islamic army was effectively defeated in the Battle of Las Navas de Tolosa. Pockets of Islam remained on the Iberian Peninsula as vassal states until Queen Isabella expelled the last of the Muslims in 1492.

The Mozarabic rite, mentioned in Chapter 1, was practiced by Christians in the Iberian Peninsula while they were under Muslim domination. The earliest surviving documents describing the rite come from Isidore of Seville (d. 636), so it predated the Muslim conquest in some form or another. At the Fourth Council of Toledo in 633, Isidore had called for unification—"one order of prayer and singing in all Spain and Gaul."[19] As the *Reconquista* proceeded, the Roman rite began to replace the Mozarabic. With the capture of Toledo in 1085, the Mozarabic rite was finally suppressed.

CODEX CALIXTINUS

The oldest edition of the Codex Calixtinus dates from about 1150 and was held in the archives of the Cathedral of Santiago de Compostela. It opens with a letter from Pope Calixtus II (r. 1119-1124) "to the very holy assembly of the basilica of Cluny" and to "Deigo, archbishop of Compostela." Scholars believe, however, that the codex was written by several authors after the death of Calixtus.

The codex has five parts. Book I contains homilies on St. James and liturgies for the celebration of his feast day. The music, found in Book I and

---

[19] See *The New Grove Dictionary of Music and Musicians* (1980), s.v. "Mozarabic rite."

appendices, contains examples of early polyphony and the first known composition for three voices. Book II recounts miracles attributed to St. James. Book III describes the transfer of St. James's body from Jerusalem to Galicia.

Book V, as discussed in the video for this unit, provides a guide for pilgrims making their way to Santiago de Compostela.

Book IV tells the history of Charlemagne and Roland, which deserves a brief explanation for it involves the intersection of Charlemagne with the *Reconquista*, the Abbasids and Umayyads, French literature, troubadours, and the Crusades. Charlemagne entered Spain in 778 and crossed the Pyrenees seeking to reclaim Christian territory after the Abbasid governor of Barcelona offered submission in return for military aid in his fight against the Umayyad Abd Al-Rahman I. This alliance was to pave Charlemagne's way into Spain, and the offer included a promise to surrender the city of Zaragoza. But things did not go as planned, Zaragoza refused to yield, and Charlemagne was forced to retreat. His knight Roland was assigned as rearguard, and as they went through Roncevaux Pass, the rearguard was attacked by the Basques and defeated.

The story would be told many times. The epic poem *Le Chanson de Roland*, composed between 1040 and 1115, is the oldest surviving work of French literature and is considered one of the best examples of the *chanson de geste* (song of heroic deeds). The story would become a favorite subject of troubadours and trouvères. And the story underwent certain revisions, in particular being recast as a battle between Charlemagne's forces and Muslims rather than against Christian Basques. The story was thus strongly identified with the Crusades and may have served as propaganda in support of the Crusades.

In the Codex Calixtinus version, St. James appears to Charlemagne in a dream, asks him to liberate his tomb from the Muslims, and gives directions by pointing him to the route of the Milky Way. Thus the Milky Way in Spain is sometimes referred to as *Camino de Santiago*.

CANTIGAS DE SANTA MARIA

The *Cantigas de Santa Maria* were assembled by Alfonso X, *el Sabio* (the Wise) who reigned as king of Castile and León from 1252 to 1284, before the official end of the Reconquista but after the last major battle. Musicologist Gustave Reese notes the consensus that this collection of over 400 songs is one of the greatest monuments of medieval music.[20] Although the poems and music likely come from many sources, Alfonso himself was quite possibly one of the authors. The *Cantigas* follow the style of the Troubadours:

> The rulers of Provence and the Iberian kingdoms frequently exchanged visits, and troubadours and *jongleurs* belonging to their entourage no doubt assisted in what might be called the cross-fertilization of the indigenous verse and music. It is not surprising, therefore, that we find a style similar to that of the troubadours in the *Cantigas de Santa Maria*.[21]

---

[20] Gustave Reese, *Music in the Middle Ages* (New York: W.W. Norton, 1968), 245.

[21] Ibid., 245.

11. The Innovative 13th Century

In the video for Unit 10, we pointed out some important events occurring around the year 1200. Among them were the compositions of Léonin and Pérotin, *Magna Carta*, and the establishment of universities. These events presaged a century of innovation in agriculture, economics, politics, and scholarship. Francis of Assisi (1182-1226) was charting a new direction for monasticism. Thomas Aquinas (1225-1274) would soon produce important intellectual milestones in Western thought. But the most tangible testament to this spirit of innovation was the sudden rise of massive cathedrals built in the new Gothic style.

GOTHIC CATHEDRALS

St. Denis, the 3rd-century bishop of Paris, was martyred after Emperor Decian in 250 A.D. ordered everyone in the empire to make a sacrifice to the Roman gods. Executed on the highest spot in Paris, now known as Montmartre (martyr's mountain), he is said to have picked up his decapitated head and walked six miles, preaching repentance along the way.

A shrine erected on the spot where he finally died developed into the Basilica of St. Denis. Denis became the patron saint of France and the shrine at St. Denis a major pilgrimage destination. The church was refounded in the 7th century by King Dagobert as a Benedictine monastery. It was selected as the burial site for French monarchs, perhaps as early as the 6th century. It housed royal documents and official histories. The abbey was granted independence from the jurisdiction of the bishop of Paris, and it flourished under royal patronage and privileges.

King Louis VI (the "fat") convened a royal assembly at St. Denis in 1124 in an attempt to rally the various feudal factions against the threat of invasion by the combined forces of Henry I of England and the Holy Roman Emperor Henry V. Abbot Suger presided as St. Denis' relics were brought out of the crypt and King Louis prayed for protection of the realm. Louis promised great gifts to the abbey if his prayers were answered. The feudal lords stood with the king; the invasion never came. From that time on, the sacred banner of the Abbey of St. Denis, the *oriflamme*, became the battle standard of the King of France.

Louis VI made good on his promise, providing priceless jewels and ordering the return of important relics that had been redistributed. Abbot Suger channeled these new gifts into the reconstruction of his deteriorating abbey. Work on the west front began in 1137 and then on the choir in 1144. Robert Scott's history of the Gothic cathedral explains Suger's vision:

> The person who actually drew up the design of the building is unknown, but it seems clear that Suger provided the inspiration. Borrowing innovations in building design from Sens and elsewhere in the provinces of northern France, Suger worked with his master mason to create a design that would embody his theological and political vision. The theological vision was of an interior space where people could glimpse heaven. Consistent with his view of heaven, his great church was to be geometrically regular, orderly, coherent, enduring, and filled with light. It would symbolize a place where diverse and seemingly contradictory forces and elements could be reconciled under one all-embracing canopy. The structure would provide a place for all things, bringing into ultimate harmony discordant forms and elements, as he imaged Divine Order did, subsuming them neatly within a singled, overarching geometrical order. . . . His design can also be seen as reflecting an effort to reconcile the antagonistic factions of France under a single roof, providing a place where all of France could rally round its patron saint and king.[22]

This first Gothic cathedral set off an avalanche of building projects, particularly in the Paris basin. Renovations of Romanesque churches began at Sens (1140), Senlis (1151), Notre Dame de Paris (1160). Competition ensued to see who could build the biggest, the tallest, the grandest. Gothic architecture

---

[22] Robert A. Scott, *The Gothic Enterprise: A Guide to Understanding the Medieval Cathedral*. E-book, University of California Press, 2011 [Ch. 5].

in somewhat modified style took root in England, notably to rebuild the fire-damaged Canterbury Cathedral in 1174, and spread quickly throughout Europe.

INNOVATIONS IN NOTATION

We saw in previous chapters how pitch notation evolved from neumes providing a rather unspecific indication of melodic contour and direction into a system of lines and spaces that conveyed precise pitches. While the rhythm of the chant was determined by the text, there was no need to develop a systematic approach to notating rhythm. Polyphony changed this. Once two voices were sounding simultaneously, they needed to be coordinated with one another.

When organum began with two voices singing the same text in parallel or oblique motion, the rhythm of the text still controlled the pulse of the melodies. The two voices would progress from note to note in the same rhythm, albeit on different pitches. With melismatic organum, this coordination between the higher, extended melismas and the lower sustained notes in the tenor presented no real difficulty. Anyone singing the tenor voice simply had to pay attention to the higher organal voice to know when to move to the next note. A visual alignment of the two voices on the page provided sufficient information.

But rhythms became more complex and fixed. Metrical rhythmic patterns, as opposed to the text's rhythm, began to control the pulse of the music. You can hear this clearly in the music of Léonin and Pérotin. Léonin established a set of rhythmic modes that mirrored poetic rhythms and were essentially six different patterns of long (*longae*) and short (*breve*) note values.

Mode I:	L B L B
Mode II:	B L B L
Mode III:	L B B
Mode IV:	B B L
Mode V:	L L
Mode VI:	B B B B B B

Patterns continued to be based on groups of three, which had theological significance. In modern notation, we would indicate these patterns where the beat is divided by three as compound (6/8) meter.

To indicate which rhythmic mode was to be sung, Léonin grouped two- and three-note patterns together using *ligatures*.

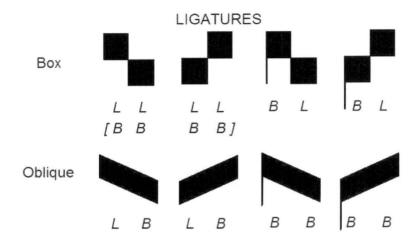

Musical works generally employed a single rhythmic mode. A change from one rhythmic mode to another was possible, but would take place only where a rest occurred. A composer could also call for some variations within the rhythmic mode, and these could be notated, as in the example above, using a stem or tail attached to the note head.

MAGNUS LIBER ORGANI

The *Magnus Liber Organi de gradali et antifonario* or "great book of organum for the gradual and antiphoner," dating from about 1170, is the principal surviving collection of two-voice polyphony from the Notre Dame School. It exists in today in three versions that differ from one another.

Anonymous IV is presumed to have been an English student at the University of Paris who, in about 1280 (some 100 years after Léonin), wrote a treatise on music of the Notre Dame School. It is through this treatise that we have information on Léonin and Pérotin. He acquired the designation Anonymous IV much later when his treatise appeared as the fourth in a series of anonymous treatises published by the French musicologist Edmond de Coussemaker.

Anonymous IV explains (and names) Léonin and Pérotin and is the most authoritative source on them. It also describes Franco of Cologne and Johannes de Garlandia.

Magnus Liber Organi

FRANCONIAN NOTATION

Franco of Cologne described the musical practices of Léonin and Pérotin in his treatise *Ars cantus mensurabilis* (c. 1250). This practical guide is important in explaining the rhythmic modes and various forms of organum in a systematic way. But Franco made a more significant contribution by advancing the idea that the duration of notes (their rhythmic value) should be specified by their individual shapes. Whereas duration within the system of rhythmic modes had depended on how the notes were grouped, note values determined by their shape provided a more objective measure. The system, called *mensural notation*, defined the durational values of individual notes in relation to each other. In other words, the shape of each note conveyed mathematically specific information about its duration. This approach made the more complex rhythms of the motet (*see below*) possible and provided the basis for our modern rhythmic notation.

THE MOTET

The New Grove Dictionary of Music and Musicians (the most authoritative English-language encyclopedia on music) has this to say about the motet: "No single set of characteristics serves to define it generally, except in particular historical or regional contexts."[23] In other words, the term *motet* was applied to different types of compositions, and varied according to time and place. And so to be precise the term generally needs one or more adjectives, *e.g.* sacred or secular, medieval or renaissance, English or French.

The term "motet" comes from the French "*mot*" (word) and seems to have developed first from the organum of Léonin and Pérotin at Notre Dame. Notre Dame organum typically featured a tenor voice singing a plainchant melody in long, sustained notes and a fast-moving organal voice above the tenor, singing many notes in a repeated rhythmic pattern (rhythmic mode). Two important innovations came along. Rhythm was added to the tenor, or sustained, voice, and a separate text was added to the organal voice.[24] Thus, the upper part, the organal voice that had been melismatic, became syllabic. Suddenly, the possibility arose of singing two texts simultaneously.

Initially the texts added to the upper voice paraphrased the text of the tenor, the type of elaboration we see in *Alle Psalite* sung by the Ring Around Quartet in the Unit 10 video. Not surprisingly (given the human love of decoration), the texts in the upper voice soon took on a life of their own, often obscuring the original text of the Gregorian melody, the Latin *cantus firmus*, in the tenor. Motets began to appear with even more voices added above the tenor, further obscuring the clarity of the text, and the additional voices soon presented texts that had nothing to do with the original text in the tenor. In short, a sacred *cantus firmus* could be decorated by upper voices that had secular texts and be overshadowed by those upper voices.

The next development saw the addition of French texts in the upper voices that were often secular instead of sacred. A French love song might be joined with a Latin hymn to the Virgin Mary.

What should we make of this mingling of sacred and secular? First, the secular texts were not intended for singing in church, so this should not necessarily be viewed as an introduction of secular elements into worship. It

---

[23] *The New Grove Dictionary of Music and Musicians* (1980), s.v. "Motet."

[24] Reese, 311.

might be more useful to view this not as profaning a sacred work, but just the opposite. As musicologist Albert Seay suggests, it demonstrates "the medieval reverence for reliance on authority."[25]

Composers of the time generally did not create music out of whole cloth for the purpose of self-expression; they elaborated on pre-existing sacred materials, and the early secular motets continued to employ sacred text and melodies as the foundation in the tenor voice. In the latter part of the 13th century, however, composers would begin to take their tenors from secular sources as well.[26]

This course of development for the 13th-century French motet illustrates historical facts relevant to our discussion in this course. It shows polyphony moving into the world of secular music and demonstrates that learned composers were now applying their skills to the creation of secular works.

---

[25] Albert Seay, *Music in the Medieval World* (Englewood Cliffs: Prentice-Hall, 1965), 112.

[26] Ibid., 117.

12. The Turbulent 14th Century

I seems that just about everything went right in the 13th century, and everything went wrong in the 14th. That is an exaggeration to be sure, but the two centuries present a stark contrast. The 13th century was characterized by growth and prosperity. The 14th saw famine, plague, schism, economic crises, and a seemingly interminable "Hundred Years" war.

In music, we sometimes apply the term *Ars antiqua* to the 13th century and *Ars nova* to the 14th. The treatise *Ars nova notandi* by Philippe de Vitry (c. 1322) explained some revolutionary changes in musical notation. Music theorists of the time were aware of the divide and made reference to the former practice associated with Franco of Cologne as *Ars antiqua*. Music of Italy in the 14th century is often given the separate designation of *Trecento*, which means "300" in Italian but is short for *mille trecento* or the 1300s (14th century).

PHILIPPE DE VITRY

Franco of Cologne had advanced a system of mensural notation in which the durational value of notes was represented by their shape (*see Unit 11*). Philippe de Vitry made further advances in mensural notation that found their way into our modern notation.

The rhythmic modes of the *Ars antiqua* had all been based on ternary divisions (the *longa* would be divided into three *breves*). This was not specified in the notation, but understood; it reflected the idea based on the Trinity which puts forth three as the perfect number. Binary rhythms were thus "imperfect." Perfect rhythm today is generally spoken of as compound meter, and imperfect rhythm as simple meter. We represent ternary divisions with dotted notes and use time signatures such as 6/8. Toward the end of the 13th century, the use of imperfect or binary rhythm for sacred music gained wider acceptance, particularly in England.

Philippe de Vitry leveled the playing field with a system that allowed either binary or ternary divisions of the notes at multiple levels: the division of longa into brevis (*modus*) and the division of brevis into semibrevis (*tempus*), and the division of semibrevis into minima (*prolatio*). All of these symbols and terminology show us just how complicated the rhythmic construction of the era's new music was becoming.

Philippe de Vitry's treatise omits any reference to perfect rhythms being superior to imperfect ones. The binary and ternary divisions were represented by time signatures.[27] Dots were also placed after notes to change their duration or to indicate syncopations. It would take some time for these features to be standardized, but they all still exist in our modern notation today.

Isorhythmic Motets

The advances in mensural notation may be seen as necessary for the greater rhythmic complexity found in the *Ars nova* motets. By the same token, composers who wanted to write works with such rhythmic complexity were forced to derive new ways to notate what they wanted. Just as composers in the 20th century who explored radical changes in music largely devised their own notation, we can assume that 14th-century composers facing a similar challenge did the same. More complex compositions drive advancements in notation, and vice versa.

Composers do not seek only novelty and complexity; they seek musical coherence and elements of unity within their works. The need for unity is obvious in works of visual art but not always apparent to those with only a casual acquaintance with music. Musical structures are built primarily with repetition of certain elements, contrasting materials, and repetition with variations. As musical works expand in length, the need for unifying principles increases.

Isorhythm can be understood as a method for extending a musical idea. To extend a work into a longer form, the *cantus firmus* often needed to

---

[27] The *modus* was shown with a rectangle that included two or three dashes. A circle placed on the staff represented ternary divisions of the *tempus* and a semicircle represented binary divisions. Students of this course need not understand the system fully, but those who know modern time signatures will see the parallels. Our 9/8 signature would correspond to ternary *modus* and *tempus*; our 3/4 to ternary *modus* and binary *tempus*; our 6/8 to binary *modus* and ternary *tempus*; our 2/4 to binary *tempus* and *modus*.

be repeated. Isorhythm involves repetition with a particular kind of variation. It is based on viewing a melody as two independent components: (1) a set of pitches (known as *color*), and (2) a set of durational values (known as *talea*—"cutting"). Each note of a melody has both. If the *color* and *talea* have the same number of elements, then the repetition would be literal. But if one has more than the other, for example 12 notes in the *color* and only 10 in the *talea*, then the repetitions will not coincide. Each repetition will generate a somewhat different combination of pitch and rhythm, achieving both unity and variety. The extent to which the listener perceives the unity is another question.

Isorhythmic motets rose to a position of prominence in the secular music of the French *Ars nova*. This is seen particularly in the *Roman de Fauvel* (1316), a long allegorical poem critical of the church. The manuscript includes 34 polyphonic compositions, some dating back to the late 13th century. Another collection, the Ivrea Codex (c. 1360), contains an interesting mix of sacred and secular works—Mass sections, motets and other secular works. There are no attributions in the codex itself, but some of the works have been attributed to Philippe de Vitry and Guillaume de Machaut.

ARS NOVA IN SACRED MUSIC

The Ivrea Codex and another codex from the town of Apt are both associated with the Avignon papacy. Little is know about the artistic environment at Avignon early in the 14th century, but there was a thriving musical life there in during the papacy of Clement VI who was a great admirer of the *Ars nova* style. Clement cultivated a coterie of musicians, including Philippe de Vitry. The Ivrea and Apt Codices show a trend toward setting the Ordinary of the Mass. Prior to this time, most polyphonic settings had focused on the Proper. The motet provided a model for this new interest in setting the Ordinary, although certain modifications were necessary to take the form from a secular to a sacred context.

The 14th century also saw a move toward joining polyphonic settings of parts of the Ordinary into a unified work. Guillaume de Machaut is credited as the first to compose a complete setting of the Ordinary in his *Messe de Nostre Dame*. But other collections, although not composed by a single person, were grouped to achieve some liturgical unity.

In the 15th century, it became common for composers to set the entire Mass Ordinary with a unified theme. These *cyclical* settings would be based on a *cantus firmus*, usually a Gregorian chant. But later, composers would begin turning to secular songs to use as a *cantus firmus* in Mass settings.

ARS SUBTILIOR

We explore in the video how the intellectual possibilities in composition and the increasing complexity of music brought about abrupt changes in musical style. This pattern shows up multiple times in music history: a style begins with simplicity and becomes increasing complex and elaborate until it collapses. This cycle runs through sacred and secular music alike. Sacred music is sometimes subject to other forces as well. Complexity in sacred music may lead to a reform movement in which the church seeks to restore clarity of purpose to the music that accompanies worship. And as secular influences creep into sacred music, efforts may be taken to eradicate them. But sacred music, like all of the arts, responds to social influences and follows the tides of cultural history.

Albert Seay, noting the turmoil at end of 14th century leading to the end of the medieval period and the diminished authority of the Church, concluded:

> With such a state of affairs, it can be no surprise that the music of the late fourteenth and early fifteenth centuries has little artistic validity or inspiration. An artistic situation in which the goals of a previous civilization and its social stability have been discarded, but without the introduction of new ideals and functions or an established social order, could but lead to sterility and formalism, particularly in music, where the connections between form and function had, in medieval times, been so close. Feeling no aesthetic goal for his creations nor a secure place in a stable society, the composer of the closing years of the century retreated into technical complexity, with little more than this to distinguish his music.[28]

Many scholars would quarrel with that rather dismal assessment of music at the end of the Middle Ages, but Seay has some strong arguments in his favor. New ideals and a new established order would be created, but something was being lost. And while we moderns tend to view the Renaissance as a welcome exit from the "Dark Ages,"

---

[28] Seay, 169.

There is much in the Middle Ages that we may admire and even envy. Society as a whole was fixed and stable, and within it most people could find contentment. They knew the rules imposed by civil authority and the church. They were not assailed by futile questionings and anxieties. Probably their mental health was better than ours. An English yeoman, a German burgher, an Italian craftsman, could lead a rewarding if unexciting life. Those who asked something more could pursue honor, join a crusade, die nobly in battle for their liege lord. Or they could renounce the world, practice asceticism and mortification of the flesh, count on a sure reward in heaven. People's faith was secure; they had a sense of closeness to God and the saints. And the saints, at least, were close to people, only a few miles or yards overhead, ready with miracles, attentive to prayers, grateful for offerings, totally occupied with people's welfare.[29]

CONCLUSION

A study entitled *Early Sacred Music* has to encompass everything from geography to economics. The musical expression of worshipping God does not spring forth within four walls, nor does it stay within them. As today, when pop styles influence Christian music, the world and its influence was very much present throughout the development of our early sacred repertoire. And that early sacred repertoire continues to have a profound influence on music and liturgies today, even when we don't know it or acknowledge it as part of our heritage.

That body of sacred music is a treasure. We celebrate its roots in the musical systems of ancient civilizations and in the practices of the Hebrew Temple and synagogues. We see how geopolitical and technological developments influenced everything from monastic structures to musical notation. And we know, from our perspective, that the enormous changes this music experienced up to the dawn of the Renaissance would not end. The great schism between the Roman church and those who rose in protest (Protestants) would lead to a focus on congregational singing (hymns) in both branches. Particularly within the Protestant movement, a new style that we call "the chorale" would explode in popularity, and it, in and of itself, was powerful enough to cause a host of developments in the secular music that surrounded

---

[29] Morris Bishop, *The Middle Age* (Boston: Houghton Mifflin, 1996), 324.

it. Could St. Ambrose have envisioned how the hymns he brought to the West would flourish?

Today, we can celebrate the unified story of our sacred musical traditions. But historically, each change was a battle, bringing in new elements or forcing limited systems to expand. The danger today is that we forget these centuries—millennia, really—of traditions. We think somehow that we don't "need" the full story, or that it has no message for us in our modern world.

The "old" names like Charlemagne and Boethius were not old in their times. They were electric personalities whose bold innovations might cause the common man to furrow his brows with worry as to where it all would lead! Yet, some of the extraordinary developments happened in the quietest of monastic cells or on the dark roads to a pilgrimage destination like Santiago de Compostela. The same can be said about the many musical and liturgical terms you have encountered in this course. They may seem off-putting, complex, or obscure upon first encounter, but they were just as cutting-edge in their time as words like "Bluetooth" and "app" are today.

Gregorian chant can be heard in many churches every Sunday. It belongs not to history, but to us. Contemporary composers incorporate it into their works, as they always have. They recognize that sung liturgy remains one of the most expressive forms of music and that its enormous possibilities for development will never be exhausted. Isaiah tells us that the angels never tire of singing the *Sanctus*.

St. Augustine may have issued the most powerful statement about sacred music: "To Sing is to Pray Twice." Remembering this dictum, regardless of its origin, will remind us both of the power of our sacred singing and of our need to understand its essence.

We are so fortunate to have resources in text, audio, and video recordings that have never been more plentiful or accessible. May these resources, and this course, ignite a life-long journey for you, and may they bring beauty and Divine inspiration beyond measure.

WHO'S WHO

Albert the Great (Albertus Magnus) (1206-1280). Saint; Dominican Friar; Bishop. Taught at University of Paris. Teacher of Thomas Aquinas.

Alcuin of York (c. 735-834). Educator and theologian. Recruited by Charlemagne to set up the palace school at Aachen, which became the center of knowledge and culture for the whole kingdom. At the center of liturgical reforms under Charlemagne.

Alexander the Great (356-323 B.C.). Macedonian king. Educated by Aristotle. Led the Greeks in the conquest of Persia and conquered territory as far east as India, establishing the primacy of Greek culture (Hellenization) throughout the eastern Mediterranean and former Persian Empire.

Alexei Romanov (1629-1676). Tsar of Russia. Second in the line of the Romanov dynasty and father of Peter the Great. Responsible, before his more famous son, for opening Russia to Western influence and courting European diplomatic, economic, and artistic connections.

Alfonso X ("the Wise") (1221-1284). King of Castille and Leon. Author of the *Cantigas de Santa Maria* written in Troubadour style. Played a significant role in the development of Spanish law.

Anonymous IV. Thought to be a student from England working at Notre Dame in Paris in the 1270s or 1280s, he wrote a treatise in music theory that is the main source for understanding the music of the School of Notre Dame.

Anthony the Great (251-356). Saint. Known as the Father of All Monks. Gave away his wealth as a young man and went to live alone in the Egyptian desert where he established a model for hermitic monastic life.

Aristotle (384-322 B.C.). Greek philosopher. Student of Plato; teacher of Alexander the Great. Known as the Father of Logic. Had a strong influence on Christian theology, particularly through the writings of Thomas Aquinas.

Athanasius of Alexandria (c. 296-373). Saint; Church Father; Bishop of Alexandria. Led the fight against the Arian heresy. Known in the Eastern Orthodox Church as the Father of Orthodoxy. Biographer of St. Anthony the Great.

Augustine of Canterbury (d. 604). Saint; Archbishop of Canterbury. Founder of the English Church. Sent by Pope Gregory the Great to evangelize England.

Augustine of Hippo (354-430). Saint; Church Father; Bishop of Hippo Regius. One of the most important Christian theologians and philosophers. Author of many important works including *The City of God* and *Confessions*.

Bede the Venerable (672-735). Saint; Doctor of the Church; Monk. The Father of English History. Author of *The Ecclesiastical History of the English People*.

Benedict of Nursia (480-547). Saint; Abbot. Author of the Rule of St. Benedict and founder of the Order of St. Benedict (OSB). Abbot of Monte Cassino.

Bernard of Clairvaux (1090-1153). Saint; Doctor of the Church; Abbot. Important in the founding of the Cistercian Order and a leading intellect of the time.

Boccaccio, Giovanni (1313-1375). Italian Writer; Poet. Author of *The Decamaron*, and important literary work in the vernacular and historical record of the physical and social effects of The Black Death.

Boethius (480-524). Roman Senator; Consul; Philosopher; Music Theorist. His significant acumen brought into the service of Emperor Theodoric where he was caught up in political intrigue. He was imprisoned and executed. During his imprisonment he wrote *Consolation of Philosophy*, which became one of the most popular books in the Middle Ages. In his musical treatise *De institutione musica*, he formulated three classifications of music: *musica universalis, musica human,* and *music instrumentalis.*

Boniface (c. 675-754). Saint. Leading figure in the Anglo-Saxon evangelization of Germanic regions of the Frankish Empire. Known as the Apostle of Germania and as the chief fomenter of the alliance between the papacy and the Carolingian family.

Caesar Augustus (63 B.C. – 14 A.D.). Founder of the Roman Empire. Born Gaius Octavianus, his maternal great uncle, Julius Caesar, adopted him and named him as his heir.

Cecilia (2nd century A.D.) Saint. The patron saint of musicians, iconography usually depicts her with an organ or other instrument. Gave financial support to the early church. She was martyred at her home in the Trastevere section of Rome.

Charlemagne (Charles Magnus, Charles the Great, Karl der Grosse) (742/747?-814). King of the Franks; Holy Roman Emperor. Known as the Father of Europe. United and expanded the Frankish Kingdom and set in motion the Carolingian Renaissance, promoting education, writing, and standardization of the Liturgy.

Charles Martel (c. 688-741). Prince of the Franks; Mayor of the Palace. Led the decisive Frankish victory at the Battle of Tours ending the last great invasion of Muslims into France. Father of Pepin and Grandfather of Charlemagne.

Clement VI (1291-1352). Pope (r. 1342-1352). The fourth of the Avignon popes and pope during the time of the Black Death, he issued two papal bulls condemning violence against the Jews and denouncing those who blamed the Jews for the Black Death. Known as a devotee of the arts who kept composers and music theorists close to him throughout his pontificate.

Clovis I (c. 466-511). King of the Franks. First to unite the Frankish tribes under one ruler. Converted to Catholicism (from Arianism) in 496, leading to widespread conversions among the people and religious unification in Europe.

Constantine (c. 272-337). Emperor of the Roman Empire. The first Christian emperor of Rome. He was responsible for building early Christian churches, notably the Church of the Holy Sepulcher in Jerusalem and Old St. Peter's in Rome.

Constantius I (c. 250-306). Joint Emperor of the Roman Empire (with Galerius). Father of Constantine.

Cyril (826-869) and **Methodius** (815-885). Saints; Theologians; Missionaries. Brothers known as the Apostles to the Slavs. They devised the Glagolitic alphabet used to transcribe Old Church Slavonic.

Cyrus the Great (d. 530 B.C.) King of the Persian Empire. Cyrus expanded the empire and conquered lands from the Mediterranean to the Indus River. Known as the King of the Four Corners of the World. Ended the Jewish exile, allowing Jews to return to the Promised Land.

Dante Alighieri (1265-1321). Italian Poet. Author of *The Divine Comedy*, describing Dante's journey through Hell, Purgatory, and Paradise and written in Italian. Known as the Father of the Italian Language.

David (c. 1040 B.C. – 970 B.C.) King of the United Kingdom of Israel. Warrior, poet and musician credited as author of many of the Psalms.

Diocletian (244-311). Roman Emperor (r. 284-305). Known for establishing the Tetrarcy, which divided the Roman Empire into East and West and for instigating the last and bloodiest persecution of Christians in the empire.

Dufay, Guillaume (c. 1397-1474). Franco-Flemish Composer. A leading figure in the Burgundian school of composition.

Egeria (dates unknown). Pilgrim; Author. Lady Egeria is purported to the be the author of *The Pilgrimage of Etheria*, an account of her pilgrimage in the 380s to the Holy Land. It is the earliest such account.

Eleanor of Aquitaine (1137-1204). Duchess of Aquitaine; Queen Consort of England. Granddaughter of William IX, Duke of Aquitaine, wife of Henry II, mother of King Richard I and King John. She is credited with promoting the literary concept of Courtly Love and planting it in England.

Elizabeth of Hungary (1207-1231). Saint; Princess of Hungary; Landgravine of Thuringia. Married at the age of 14 to Louis IV of Thuringia. Lived at Wartburg Castle. Subject of the Miracle of the Roses.

Franco of Cologne (fl. mid 13th century). German Music Theorist. Author of *Ars cantus mensurabilis*, which argued that rhythmic values in music should be indicated by their appearance on the page and not merely from context.

Galerius (260-311). Joint Emperor of the Roman Empire (with Constantius). Reigned 293-305 as Caesar under Diocletian and 305-311 as Augustus. Ended the Diocletian Persecution with an edict of toleration in 311.

Giotto di Bondone (d. 1337). Italian Painter and Architect. Considered the first great artist of the Renaissance. Painter of the Arena Chapel in Padua and designer of the *campanile* (bell tower) of the Florence Cathedral.

Goths. Eastern Germanic peoples, which included the Visigoths and Ostrogoths that played an important role in the Fall of Rome.

Gregory the Great (c. 540-604). Saint; Pope (r. 590-604); Doctor of the Church. First pope from a monastic background. Made significant reforms to the Liturgy. The standardized body of Roman Rite chant was subsequently attributed to him, but that is primarily a matter of legend. Sent Augustine of Canterbury to evangelize England.

Gregory VII (c. 1015-1085). Saint; Pope (r. 1073-1085). Established papal supremacy after prolonged conflict with Henry IV.

Guido of Arezzo (991/992-after 1033). Italian Music Theorist; Monk. Regarded as the inventor of staff notation to replace neumatic notation. Created a mnemonic device known as the Guidonian hand for the solmization system (do, re, mi, etc) based on the hymn *Ut quaent laxis*.

Hadrian (76-138). Emperor of the Roman Empire. Known as one of the "five good emperors." Suppressed the Bar Kokhba revolt and expelled Jews and Christians from Jerusalem.

Helena (248-328). Saint; Empress. Mother of Constantine. Traveled to the Holy Land in 326-28 to identify holy sites and to discover relics.

Henry II (1133-1189). King of England. Married Eleanor of Aquitaine with whom he had eight children, including King Richard I and King John. His desire to reform relations with the Church led him into conflict with Thomas Becket. After complaining "Will no one rid me of this meddlesome priest," Becket was murdered in Canterbury Cathedral.

Henry V (1387-1422). King of England. Victor at the Battle of Agincourt in 1415.

Henry VIII (1491-1547). King of England (r. 1509-1547). Known for his role in separating the Church of England from papal authority, making himself the head of the Church of England, and for the Suppression of the Monasteries in which the Benedictine monastic life was eradicated and its property confiscated.

Herod the Great (c. 74 B.C.-4 B.C.). King of Judea. Herod obtained his crown from the Roman Senate and thus was a vassal of Rome. Known for the ambitious expansion of the Second Temple. Also known for the Massacre of the Innocents (Matthew 2:1-23).

Hildegard von Bingen (1098-1179). Saint; Doctor of the Church; Abbess; Composer. Known for her liturgical drama *Ordo virtutum*. Also known for her scientific writings and as a Christian mystic who experienced many visions that were recorded in her writings.

Huns. A group of nomadic people who lived in Eastern Europe and Central Asia between the first and seventh centuries. They formed a unified empire under Attila. Their migration westward may have triggered the Great Migration that contributed to the fall of the Roman Empire.

Ivan Vasisyevich (1547-1584) ("Ivan IV," also "Ivan the Terrible"). Tsar of Russia. Last powerful ruler in the first dynasty of Russian tsars (Riuriks).

Oversaw the building of St. Basil's Cathedral on the Kremlin Square and famously blinded its architect.

James the Apostle (d. 44 A.D.). James, son of Zebedee, was one of the Twelve Apostles. He is thought to be the first apostle martyred. Brother of John the Apostle. According to legend, his bones are enshrined at Santiago de Compostela in northwestern Spain.

Joan of Arc (1412-1431). Saint. Came to prominence through divine visions concerning the conduct of the Hundred Years' War with England. Under her leadership the siege of Orléans was lifted in 1429 and the tide of war turned. After being captured by pro-English Burgundians, she was tried for heresy and burned at the stake.

John Cassian (c. 360-c. 435). Saint; Monk. A monastic in Bethlehem and Egypt, he later went to Rome and accepted an invitation to establish a monastery in southern Gaul. His writings influenced Benedict, who incorporated Cassian's principles into the Rule of St. Benedict. Known for bringing the ideas and practices of Christian monasticism in Egypt into medieval Europe.

John Chrysostom (c. 349-407). Saint; Father of the Church; Archbishop of Constantinople. His writings had a strong influence on the Catechism of the Catholic Church and are particularly important in Eastern Christianity. His revisions of the prayers and rubrics of the Divine Liturgy are thought to form the liturgy typically used by Eastern Orthodox and Byzantine Rite Catholics.

John of Bohemia ("the blind") (1296-1346). King of Bohemia. Killed at the Battle of Crécy. Employer of Machaut.

Josephus (37-c. 100). Roman-Jewish Scholar and Historian. Fought against the Romans in the First Roman-Jewish War until he surrendered in 67. He was kept by Emperor Vespasian as an interpreter and later freed. His writings *The Jewish War* and *Antiquities of the Jews* provide an important history of the 1st century and early Christianity.

Julius Caesar (100 B.C. – 44 B.C.). Dictator of Rome. Led military expeditions to Gaul and Britain, expanding Roman territory. Defied the Senate by crossing the Rubicon and entering Rome with his legions in 49 B.C. Assumed control of the government and was proclaimed "dictator in perpetuity." He was assassinated by a group of Senators led by Brutus, setting of a series of civil wars in which Octavian (Caesar Augustus) ultimately prevailed.

Landini, Francesco (1325-1397). Italian Composer. Foremost proponent of the *Trecento* style (Italian *Ars nova*). Wrote secular music almost entirely.

Léonin (1150-1201). Composer. First composer of polyphonic organum whose identity is known. Earliest known member of the Notre Dame School, composing in the *Ars antiqua* style of polyphony. Named by Anonymous IV as the composer of the *Magnus liber organi* (big book of organum).

Liszt, Franz (1811-1886). Composer; Pianist; Conductor; Teacher. His oratorio *Christus* (1872) begins with the Advent chant *Rorate coeli*, and is an example of the continued use of plainchant into more modern times.

Lombards. A tribe of Germanic from Scandinavia that migrated to northwestern Germany in the 1st century and to the Danube by the 5th century. After the debilitating Gothic Wars of 535-554 between Byzantium and the Ostragothic Kingdom in Italy, the Lombards invaded Italy almost unopposed. Made up primarily of pagans and Arian Christians, they did not have good relations with Rome. Charlemagne, in aid of the pope, defeated the Lombards in 774.

Louis IX (1214-1270). Saint; King of France (r. 1226-1270). Participated in the Seventh and Eighth Crusades. Patron of the Arts and innovator in Gothic architecture.

Machaut, Guillaume de (1300-1377). French Poet and Composer; Canon. Secretary to King John of Bohemia, he accompanied the king on his journeys. Known for his lyric poetry reflecting the conventions of courtly love and musical compositions in the *Ars nova* style, primarily secular in nature. His *Messe de Nostre Dame* is the first complete setting of the Ordinary by a single composer conceived as a unit.

Maxentius (c. 278-312). Emperor of the Roman Empire (r. 306-312). Son of Maximian. Began construction of the Basilica of Maxentius in the Roman Forum, an example of basilica architectural form adapted for use in early Christian churches. Constantine completed the basilica after defeating Maxentius at the Battle of Milvian Bridge.

Maximian (c. 250-305). Emperor of the Roman Empire (r. 285 or 286-305). Father of Maxentius. Co-emperor with Diocletian.

Methodius. *See Cyril and Methodius.*

Pachomius (292-348). Saint; Abbot. Known as the founder of Christian cenobitic monasticism. Became a hermitic monk to imitate St. Anthony until he heard a voice telling him to build a dwelling for hermitic monks. Established a community of monks living together in which their property was held in common under the leadership of an abbot.

Paul the Deacon (c. 720s-799). Historian; Monk. Monk at Monte Cassino. Author of *History of the Lombards*. Gained Charlemagne's notice and became a force in the Carolingian Renaissance. The hymn *Ut quaent laxis* is attributed to him.

Pepin ("the Short") (714-768). King of the Franks (r. 751-768). Father of Charlemagne; son of Charles Martel. As Mayor of the Palace, Pepin had the effective power of the realm but not the title. The king had the title, but no power. Pepin appealed to the pope whether this was the proper state of things and, with the pope's blessing, was the first of the Carolingian line to be crowned king.

Pérotin (fl. c. 1200). Composer. Member of the Notre Dame School, composing in the *Ars antiqua* style of polyphony. Successor of Léonin. Described by Anonymous IV as "Pérotin the Master."

Peter the Great (1672-1725). Tsar of Russia. Known for his reforms introducing many Western influences and moving the capital to his newly constructed city of St. Petersburg.

Petrarch (Francesco Petrarca) (1304-1374). Italian Scholar; Poet. Known as Father of the Renaissance. His works (along with those of Boccaccio and Dante) formed the basis for the modern Italian language.

Philippe de Vitry (1291-1361). French Composer; Music Theorist; Poet; Bishop. Author of the treatise *Ars nova notandi*, which gave the name to the *Ars nova* era. Served in the papal retinue of Pope Clement VI. Became Bishop of Meaux in 1351.

Plato (428/427 or 424/423 B.C.-348/347 B.C.) Greek Philosopher. Considered the most pivotal figure in the development of philosophy. His philosophical writings informed certain aspects of early Christian thought, particularly the writings of St. Augustine.

Plotinus (c. 204-270). Greek Philosopher. Platonist known for leading what scholars would later call the Neoplatonist school. Influenced early Christian philosophies. Important in the development of aesthetics.

Pythagoras (570 B.C.-495 B.C.). Greek Philosopher; Mathematician. Known for the Pathagorean Theorem. Had a strong influence on Plato. Credited with discovering the mathematical properties of music. Posited that celestial bodies moved according to mathematical principles created a "harmony of the spheres."

Rachmaninov, Sergei (1873-1943). Russian Composer; Pianist. Among his many works are two important a cappella choral works based on Russian Orthodox liturgies: *All-Night Vigil* (Vespers) and *Liturgy of St. John Chrysostom*.

Richard I ("the Lionheart") (1157-1199). King of England. Son of Henry II and Eleanor of Aquitaine. Helped to lead the Third Crusade. Known as the Troubadour King and composer of Troubadour songs. Captured on his return from the Crusade by the Duke of Austria and held for ransom. According to folklore, his location was discovered by his minstrel who went from castle to castle singing a song and hearing Richard sing the refrain.

Rublev, Andrei (b. 1360-70, d. 1427-1430). Saint; Iconographer. His Trinity icon is regarded as the highest artistic expression of Trinitarian dogma.

Solomon (990-931 B.C.). King of Israel (r. c. 970-931). Son of King David. Builder of the First Temple in Jerusalem. (1 Kings 6).

Stalin, Joseph (1878-1953). General Secretary of the Central Committee of the Communinist Party of the Soviet Union (in office 1922-1953). Oversaw the destruction of churches in Russia.

Theodosius I ("the Great") (347-395). Emperor of the Roman Empire (r. 379-392). Issued decrees making Nicene Christianity the official church of the Roman Empire.

Thomas Aquinas (1225-1274). Saint; Doctor of the Church; Dominican Friar. An immensely influential theologian and philosopher, he embraced aspects of Aristotle's philosophy and synthesized them with Christianity. Author of the *Summa Theologica*.

Thomas Becket (1119-1170). Saint; Archbishop of Canterbury. Becket's conflict with Henry II over the rights and privileges of the Church vis-à-vis the Crown led to Becket's murder in Canterbury Cathedral. His martyrdom established Canterbury as a prominent pilgrimage site.

Titus (39-81). Emperor of Rome (r. 79-81). Military commander in the First Jewish-Roman War which ended with the destruction of the Temple in 70. Also known for completing construction of the Roman Coliseum.

Urban II (d. 1099). Pope (r. 1088-1099). Prior at the Abbey of Cluny. Known for initiating the First Crusade in 1099.

Vandals. An East Germanic tribe that came into conflict with Rome along the Danube in the 2nd century. They eventually entered Roman territory around 400. They later laid siege to the Hippo Regius in 430 at the end of Augustine's life and reached their peak of power in Sicily and North Africa in the 470s.

Visigoths. *See Goths.*

William IX (1071-1127). Duke of Aquitaine. The earliest troubadour poet whose works survive. He joined the Crusades in 1101 after the success of the First Crusade in 1099. Grandfather of Eleanor of Aquitaine.

William the Conqueror (1028-1087). King of England (r. 1066-1087). Victor in the Norman Conquest of England at the Battle of Hastings in 1066. First of the Norman line of Kings.

GLOSSARY

A cappella. Cappella in Italian means "chapel." A cappella refers to music "in the church style," meaning choral music unaccompanied by instruments.

Abbey. The buildings occupied by a community of monks or nuns, generally under the authority of an abbot. Many of the great churches of Europe are either abbeys or cathedrals.

Abbot. A term derived from the Syriac abba or Lain abatia, meaning father, an abbot is the head of a monastery. The female equivalent is abbess.

Acoustics. The physical science of sound and hearing.

Advent. Advent is the first season of the Church Year. It always begins on a Sunday and includes the four Sundays immediately preceding Christmas. So Advent will begin on whichever Sunday falls between and November 27 and December 3. Advent ends on Christmas Eve.

Aerophone. A classification of musical instruments in which the air itself forms the vibrator, e.g. flutes, reed instruments, and brass instruments. *Compare* Chordophones, Idiophones, Membranophones.

Aesthetics. The branch of philosophy that deals with the nature and appreciation of beauty.

Agnus Dei. Latin for "Lamb of God," the Agnus Dei is part of the Ordinary of the Mass sung during Communion.

Ambrosian. The repertory of chant that developed in Milan. It was named after St. Ambrose (340-397), a bishop of Milan noted for his influence on St Augustine. Ambrose is also credited with introducing hymns from the Eastern Church into the West.

Anapest. A metrical foot in poetry comprised of two unstressed syllables followed by a syllable that is stressed, e.g. "I must finish my journey alone."

Anglo-Saxon. Referring to the Germanic peoples who populated England from the 5th century A.D. to the Norman Conquest of 1066.

Aniconic. Without idols or images; opposed to the use of idols or images in worship.

Anno domini. Latin for the year of Our Lord and commonly abbreviated as A.D. The system was first devised by the Scythian monk Dionysius Exiguus in 525 and introduced by Bede the Venerable in his *Ecclesiastical History of the English People* (731).

Antiphon. A Latin chant sung as a refrain to a psalm, it was usually sung before and after the psalm and sometimes interspersed within the verses of the psalm.

Antiphonal. Music sung alternately by two groups. The term is sometimes used to mean antiphonary—a book containing a collection of antiphons.

Apostolic. Pertaining to the Twelve Apostles. Apostolic succession refers to the successive ordinations of bishops in a line that traces back to the apostles.

Apotrapaic. Having the power to avert evil.

Apse. A semicircular recess covered with a hemispherical vault or semi dome, it is typically found at the east end of a basilica or cathedral where the high altar is located.

Arch. A curved structure forming the upper edge of an open space and supporting the weight above it. Arches were used systematically by the Romans in many structures and later formed an integral component of Christian church architecture.

Archeology. The scientific study of people and their cultures through the analysis of physical materials, artifacts, inscriptions, and other remains.

Ark of the Covenant. The chest containing the two stone tablets of the Ten Commandments that was carried by the Israelites during their 40 years in the desert and that was eventually placed in the Holy of Holies when the Temple was constructed by King Solomon.

Ars antiqua. L. ancient art. A term used to describe the polyphonic music of the 12th and 13th centuries, particularly that of Léonin and Pérotin, that preceded the *Ars nova*.

Ars nova. L. new art. A term used to describe the compositional and notation techniques of the 14th century.

Ars subtillior. L. more subtle art. A term used to describe the French vocal music of the late 14th century that used complex rhythms.

Ascetic. The practice of severe self-discipline and abstention.

Augmentation. The lengthening of time values of notes. Contrast *Diminution*.

Augustus. Venerable or majestic, the title was given to Octavian, the first Roman emperor.

Aulos. A wind instrument of ancient Greece and Rome consisting of two cylindrical pipes, each with a double reed, played simultaneously by the mouth of a single musician.

Autocephalous. Self-headed, usually referring to a hierarchical church structure in which the bishop does not report to any higher authority.

Barbarian. In ancient Greece, the term was applied to non-Greek speaking peoples, and by the Greeks and Romans generally was used to refer to foreigners. The term implies a less civilized or primitive culture.

Basilica. From the Greek *stoa*, the term was used by the Romans to describe an open, public court building. It came to describe early Christian buildings with similar architectural form characterized by a central nave, side aisles, and an apse.

Bellows. A device that compresses air when squeezed, often used for blowing air onto a fire or through the pipes of an organ.

Benedictine. Referring to monastic communities that follow the Rule of St. Benedict. The Order of St. Benedict (OSB) is comprised of independent Benedictine communities.

Benedictus. Benedictus frequently refers to the Song of Zachariah [Luke 1:68-79]. In the Mass, the Benedictus comprises the second part of the Sanctus, which is sung during communion. The text, "Blessed is he that cometh in the name of the Lord," comes from Jesus's entry into Jerusalem on Palm Sunday [Matthew 21:9 and Psalm 118:26].

Black Death. A pandemic resulting in the death of an estimated 75 to 200 million people from 1346 to 1353 with several reappearances thereafter. It is generally thought to have been bubonic plague. In Europe today you will find many "plague columns" (also called Marian columns or Holy Trinity columns) that were built in thanksgiving for the end of the plague.

Black Notation. A form of mensural notation in which all of the note shapes were solid or filled-in. Beginning in the mid-15th century, hollow shapes ("white notation") were used to signify longer note values.

Buttress. A projecting support of stone or brick against a wall. A buttress resists the lateral forces pushing a cathedral wall outward. A **flying buttress** is one that is not in contact with the wall itself, but placed some distance outside the wall and supported by arches. Buttresses are characteristic of Gothic architecture and permitted the walls to be higher, thinner, and filled with windows.

Caesar. The title of the Roman emperor, Caesar (literally "hairy") was the name of Julius Caesar. The first emperor Caesar Augustus had been adopted by Julius Caesar and therefore also bore the name (Gaius Julius Caesar Octavianus). Emperors after about 68-69 A.D. began using Caesar as a title rather than merely a familial name.

Cantiga. Spanish song. The term usually refers to a 13th-century monophonic song in honor of the Virgin Mary.

Cantillation. The intoned speech used in the reading of sacred texts in Hebrew worship.

Cantus firmus. A pre-existing melody in a polyphonic musical work. The *cantus firmus* (fixed voice) was often a Gregorian chant melody that typically appeared in notes of longer duration in the lower (tenor) voice and served as the basis for the entire musical work.

Carolingian. Referring to the Frankish nobles who replaced the Merovingian line of kings when Pepin the Short was crowned with the consent of the pope in 751. The name was derived from the Latin name of Charles Martel (Carolus), the father of Pepin the Short and the grandfather of Charlemagne.

Catacombs. Subterranean passageways, specifically those used by early Christians in Rome for worship and as a place of burial.

Catechumen. Literally "one being instructed" in the Catechism, the tenets of the Christian faith, as a preparation for baptism.

Celtic Chant. The plainchant of the medieval church in Ireland, Britain, and Brittany. Established by St. Patrick in the 5th century, this form of chant moved to the European continent and was later supplanted as the Roman Rite became the standard in Carolingian times.

Chant. The intoning or singing of a text using a simple melody, often using only one note or on a primary pitch called a reciting tone. With the emphasis on the text, chant may be thought of as a stylized form of speech.

Cherubim. Winged angelic beings represented in art as a lion or bull with eagle's wings and a human face. After the Fall in Genesis, Cherubim were placed to guard the entrance to the Garden of Eden and on the mercy seat of the *Ark of the Covenant*. (Not to be confused the chubby male children known as *Putti*.)

Chi Rho. Chi and Rho are the first two letters of the Greek word Kristos (Christ). The symbol Chi Rho is formed by superimposing these two letters. Constantine had a dream before the Battle of Milvian Bridge in which he was ordered to put this symbol on his soldiers' shields.

Chivalry. Literally "horsemanship," chivalry was the religious, moral, and social code of medieval knights developed in the 12th and 13th centuries. Chivalry became the ideal for *courtly love* in the secular songs of the Troubadours and Minnesingers during the time of the Crusades.

Chordophone. A classification of musical instruments in which a string stretched between two points vibrates with a sound board or resonator attached, e.g. violins, lutes, harps, pianos. *Compare* Aerophones, Idiophones, Membranophones.

Cherubic Hymn or *Cherubikon*. The hymn sung at the point in the Eastern Orthodox liturgy and at Great Vespers (Sundays and Feast Days) where the priests enter the sanctuary through the Holy Doors. The hymn symbolizes the incorporation of those present in the liturgy with the angels gathered around God's throne.

Cistercian. A member of the Cistercian Order of monks and nuns. The name comes from the village of Cîteaux in Eastern France where the order was founded in 1098 as a reform movement to follow the Rule of St. Benedict more closely. Early influential Cistercians include Bernard of Clairvaux.

Codex. From the Latin *caudex* (tree trunk), a book comprised of bound sheets of paper, vellum, papyrus, or parchment with hand-written content.

Codex Calixtinus. A 12th-century manuscript attributed to Pope Calixtinus II but now believed to have been compiled by the French scholar Aymeric Picaud. It includes five books containing liturgies, miracle stories, history, music, and a guide for pilgrims on the Way to Santiago de Compostela.

Compline. Derived from the Latin *completorium*, Compline is the Daily Office that occurs at the end of the day.

Conductus. From the Latin *conducere* (to escort), a conductus was sung in the worship service when the lectionary was carried from its place of safekeeping to the place where it was to be read. It is associated with the Notre Dame School. It is characterized by non-liturgical texts sung in Latin (often on saints' lives). It differed from other forms of polyphony in that it was usually in a rhythmic style with all voices singing together "note-against-note."

Consonant. Being in agreement or harmony; not dissonant. Two pitches sounded together are deemed consonant if they blend pleasingly.

Contrary Motion. Melodic motion in which one part rises in pitch while the other descends.

Council of Trent. The ecumenical council of the Roman Catholic Church held between 1545 and 1563 in Trent and Bologna in response to the Protestant Reformation. The council was significant in stating general attitudes to music in worship, that it should uplift the faithful, that the words should be intelligible, and that secular influences should be avoided.

Courtly Love. The medieval literary conception of love characterized by nobility and chivalry. It was developed in the French regions of Aquitaine, Provence, Champagne and Burgundy after the first Crusade and brought to England by Eleanor of Aquitaine (1137-1204). It is the subject of many Troubadour poems, and its ideals carried over at the time into songs of Marian devotion.

Credo. A statement of faith, literally "I believe." It refers frequently to the Nicene Creed, which comprises a part of the Ordinary of the Mass.

Curia. An assembly or council in which public or religious issues are discussed and decided. A king's council was often referred to in medieval times as a curia. It also refers commonly to the council that assists the pope in governing the church.

Dactyl. A metrical foot in poetry comprised of one stressed syllable followed by two unstressed syllables, e.g. "This is the forest primeval."

Danse macabre. The dance of death. Images of *danse macabre* appeared frequently in the 14th century as result of the horrors of famine, war, and the Black Death.

Dark Ages. The historical period of the early Middle Ages, beginning with the Fall of Rome and ending (depending on the dating) either c. 800 or c. 1000. The term emphasizes the cultural and economic collapse that accompanied the fall of the Roman Empire and the lack of historical documentation that survived from the period.

Deacons' Doors. The single doors on the iconostasis that are on the left and right of the Holy Doors (middle doors). Used by the clergy most frequently when entering the altar.

Diabulus in musica. The devil in music refers to the problem of the tritone, the dissonant and unstable interval comprised of three adjacent whole steps (an augmented fourth). The tritone will inevitably appear in polyphonic music that has any melodic range, and composers devised ways to avoid it by adjusting one of the notes to form the interval of either a perfect fourth or fifth.

Diaspora. The dispersion of the Jews beyond Israel. The major events of the Jewish Diaspora are the Assyrian Exile in 733 B.C., the Babylonian Exile in 597 B.C., the destruction of the Temple in 70 A.D. (the Roman Exile), and the Bar Kokhba revolt in 132 A.D., after which Jews were forbidden to live in Jerusalem.

Didactic. Related to education and teaching. Didactic art tends to be that which conveys some truth or moral teaching. *Didactic* also contrasts with *ecstatic*, the first being restrained and learned and the second being spontaneous and emotional.

Diminution. A melodic device in which the rhythmic values of the notes are proportionally shortened. Contrast *Augmentation*.

Dissonant. Not pleasing or harmonious. Two or more notes sounded together that seem to clash. Contrast *Consonant.*

Divine Comedy. The *Divine Comedy* is an epic poem of Dante Aligheri written between 1308 and 1320 and considered the preeminent work of Italian literature. It describes Dante's journey through Hell, Purgatory, and Heaven.

Divine Liturgy. The celebration of the Eucharist in the Eastern Orthodox Church.

Ecstatic. Feeling overwhelming happiness; an experience of mystic transcendence. Ecstatic art contrasts with the didactic. *See Didactic.*

Edict. The announcement or proclamation of law given by a sovereign or monarch.

Epiphany. A manifestation; a sudden and striking realization. In the Christian Liturgical Year, Epiphany is the season that follows the twelve days of Christmas. In Western Christianity it commemorates the visitation of the Wise Men, and in Eastern Christianity it is associated with Jesus's baptism and his manifestation to the world as the Christ.

Eucharist. The Lord's Supper, the service of Bread and Wine instituted by Christ in the Upper Room on Maundy Thursday. The word itself *eukharistia* means "thanksgiving," from Greek *eukharistos* (grateful), which has the Greek word *kharis* (grace) at its root.

Exile. The state of being barred from one's native country. In biblical history, *exile* refers generally to the sacking of Jerusalem in 597 B.C. and the ensuing exile of the Jewish people to Babylon (also called the Babylonian Captivity). *See* 2 Kings 24; Psalm 137.

Feast. A day set aside for religious celebration; a day devoted to a significant event in the Christian calendar or to the commemoration of one of the saints

Filioque. Latin meaning "and the Son." The phrase appears in the version of the Nicene Creed used by Western Christians: "And in the Holy Spirit, the Lord, the giver of life, who proceeds from the Father *and the Son.*" The words "and the Son" are not placed at this point in the Orthodox rendering of the Nicene Creed. It is a major doctrinal difference between the West and East and factored strongly in the Schism of 1054.

First Temple. The Temple built during the reign of King Solomon (c. 970-931 B.C.). It housed the *Ark of the Covenant* and was the focal point of Jewish worship. It was destroyed by Nebuchadnezzar II during the Siege of Jerusalem in 597 B.C.

Folio. From the Latin word for "leaf," folio refers both to a sheet of paper or parchment and to the method of arranging sheets within a book. A book that is called a "folio" is made from sheets (leaves) that are folded once and, when printed front and back, produce four pages of the book. The resulting front and back sides of the page as bound are called the "recto" and "verso" respectively.

Fresco. A technique of mural painting executed on wet lime plaster. The pigment merges with the plaster and becomes a part of the wall.

Gallican. Gallican chant developed in the Frankish kingdom from the 5th century and was abolished by Pepin in favor of the Roman Rite. No examples of the chant survive but contemporary writings describe it a distinctive style that was inelegant compared to the Roman Rite.

Gargoyle. A carved, usually grotesque figure with a spout designed to channel rainwater away from the sides of buildings. From the French *gargouille*, meaning throat or gullet. Outside of this utilitarian function, gargoyles carved in animal form were a feature of ancient Egyptian, Greek, and Roman architecture.

Gothic architecture used gargoyles to portray evil or the battle between evil and good.

Gathering. In bookbinding, a group of sheets, folded in the middle, and bound together. In medieval manuscripts, a gathering (or *Quire*) was generally comprised of four sheets.

Gloria. Gloria in excelsis Deo (Glory to God in the Highest). A part of the Ordinary of the Mass sung after the Kyrie and before the Credo.

Goliards. Wandering scholars or clerics who wrote and disseminated Latin poems in the 10th through 13th centuries.

Gothic. A form of architecture that originated in 12th-century France and flourished in the high Middle Ages. Gothic architecture is characterized by pointed arches and flying buttresses that shifted weight away from the walls and permitted the walls to be higher and filled with windows. The first Gothic cathedral was built under the supervision of Abbot Suger at St.-Denis near Paris with the goals of adding height to the structure and admitting as much as light as possible.

Great Famine. One of a series of crises that struck Europe in the early 14th century, it coincided with the end of the Medieval Warm Period. Unusually cold and rainy weather led to crop failures in Northern Europe, peaking in 1315-1317.

Gregorian Chant. A form of chant developed in medieval times for use in Western Christian liturgy that is monophonic, unaccompanied, based on the rhythm of the text, and that has a limited vocal range. Its attribution to Pope Gregory the Great is largely a matter of legend, and it is generally accepted that it was developed in Carolingian times as a standardization of the Roman rite.

Guidonian Hand. A system developed by Guido of Arezzo to instruct singers in sightreading. Each part of the hand (joints and fingertips) signified a note and allowed singers to visualize the hexachords and the placement of half steps. The lowest pitch represented was G (*gamma*), using the syllable *ut*. Thus the term *gamut* came to signify the whole range of pitches and, later, the whole range of anything.

Hallel. A Jewish prayer or praise and thanksgiving consisting of a recitation of Psalms 113-118.

Heighted (Heightened) Neumes. A development in neumatic notation (*see Neumes*) that indicated the relative pitches between neumes by way of vertical spacing on the page. This system was a precursor to modern notation, which uses regulated vertical spacing to indicate pitch, and which led to the creation of the musical staff.

Hellenistic. Referring to the period of ancient Greek history between the death of Alexander in 323 B.C. and the beginning of the Roman Empire after the Battle of Actium in 31 B.C.

Hexachord. A group of six adjacent notes of a scale. Treatises in the Middle Ages described three hexachords, each with whole steps between all pitches except the middle two, which are separated by a half step. These hexachords could begin on G, C, or F, and each hexachord would use the syllables *ut, re, mi, fa, sol, la. See Solmization.*

High Priest. The chief religious official of Judaism in post-exilic times. The High Priest alone was permitted to enter the *Holy of Holies* exclusively on the Day of Atonement to offer the sacrifices for the sins of the people.

Holy of Holies. The inner sanctuary of the Tabernacle in the Wilderness and later the Temple where the *Ark of the Covenant* was kept.

Homophonic. Music in which one voice predominates as melodic and other voices serve as accompaniment or harmony.

Hundred Years' War. A series of conflicts between 1337-1453 between England and France for control of the French kingdom. Some of the major events in this long conflict include the Battle of Crécy (1346), the Battle of Poitiers (1356), the Battle of Agincourt (1415), the Siege of Orléans (1428) and the life of Joan of Arc (1412-1431).

Hydraulis. An early pipe organ dated from Hellenistic Greece that used water to create air pressure for the pipes. It is considered to be the earliest keyboard instrument.

Hymn. St. Augustine defines hymn as a song embodying the praise of God. Hymns were a part of Hebrew worship and were used in the Western and Eastern branches of the early Church.

Iamb. A metrical foot in poetry comprised of one unstressed syllable followed by one stressed syllable,

Iconostasis. A wall of icons in Eastern Orthodox churches that separates the nave from the sanctuary. Certain rubrics exist for the placement of the doors (*see Royal Doors* and *Deacons' Doors*) and specific icons depicting Christ, the Mother of God, apostles, patriarchs, saints, various feasts and biblical events.

Idiophone. A classification of musical instruments in which the substance of the instrument itself yields the sound by being struck or rubbed, e.g. triangles, cymbals. *Compare Aerophones, Chordophones, Membranophones.*

Illumination. A decoration in a manuscript such as elaborate and colorful initials, marginalia, and borders. The figures within the decoration often narrate stories.

Imperfect Rhythm. Rhythm in which the predominant division of the beat is binary.

Isorhythm. A compositional technique popular in the 14th century in which a rhythmic pattern (*talea*) is repeated as a main structural element of the work, and a pitch pattern (*color*) of a different length is also repeated. Because the *talea* and *color* differ in length, or number of notes, numerous melodic variations would result.

Italian *Ars nova*. Also called *trecento*, the style (associated with Francesco Landini) employed some of the notation and compositional techniques of the French *Ars nova*, but without the complexity.

Ite missa est. The versicle chanted by the Deacon at the end of the Mass as a dismissal. "Missa" came to signify the entire Eucharistic Liturgy and is the origin of the term *Mass*.

Jebusite. Referring to the Canaanite tribe that built and inhabited Jerusalem prior to its conquest by King David.

Kithara. An ancient Greek instrument in the lyre family used primarily to accompany dances, recitations, odes, and lyric songs.

Kondakarion. The earliest known form of notation for Orthodox chant. A staffless system conveyed on elaborate signs (neumes) placed above the words of the text.

Kyrie. The *Kyrie eleison* (Lord, have mercy) comprises the first part of the Ordinary of the Mass. It is the one part of the Western Mass that is in Greek rather than Latin.

Lapis Lazuli. A deep blue semi-precious stone prized for its intense color used to make pigments for manuscripts.

Lauds. The Daily Offices that occurs in the early morning hours.

Lent. The penitential season of 40 days that precedes Easter, beginning on Ash Wednesday. Many Christians take up disciplines of fasting and penance during Lent. In the liturgy, alleluias are omitted and specific religious objects (such as the crucifix and processional cross) are veiled.

Levite. A descendant of the Tribe of Levi, one of the twelve tribes of Israel. From this tribe the priests and musicians serving in the Temple were drawn. The Levites were the only tribe not given land upon the Israelites' entry into the Promised Land because the Lord God of Israel himself is their inheritance. [Deuteronomy 18:2]

Liber Usualis. Literally, the "usual book" or "common book," it is a book of Gregorian chants for many occasions compiled by monks of Solesmes Abbey in 1896.

Ligature. Something used to bind. In musical notation, ligatures were symbols that told musicians how to perform two or more notes on a single syllable. Ligatures were used in early mensural notation to signify which rhythmic mode was to be applied.

Line fillers. Scribes would often add a horizontal line after the last word where the text did not reach the right margin. In part, it prevented additional words from being added later and is similar to the modern practice of adding a line after the dollar amount when writing a check.

Liturgical Colors. The colors associated with the seasons of the Liturgical year and used in priestly vestments and altar cloths. Specific colors may vary from one tradition to the next, but among them violet is commonly used for penitential seasons of Lent and Advent, white for Christmas and Easter, red for Pentecost, and Green for Ordinary Time.

Liturgical Drama. A religious drama popular especially in the 12th and 13th centuries that presented a moral and edifying lesson through the enactment of stories originally taken from the Gospels or Office of the day. A favorite in medieval times was *Quem quaeritis?* (Whom do you seek?) the story of the angel and the three Marys at the empty tomb on Easter.

Liturgy. In Western Christianity, a general term for public religious worship; a rite or body of rites prescribed for public worship. In Eastern Christianity, the name given to the service that celebrates the Eucharist (Mass).

Liturgy of the Word. The first of two portions of the Mass made up primarily of scriptural readings, the homily, and prayers. It is followed by the Liturgy of the Eucharist or Lord's Supper.

Logogenic. Music in which the words dominate the melody. Contrast "melogenic."

Lyre. A U-shaped, plucked stringed instrument used especially in ancient Greece.

Manuscript. From the Latin *manu scriptus*, meaning written by hand. Today it tends to distinguish a document that is handwritten or typewritten as opposed to one that is printed or produced in some automated way. Medieval manuscripts were generally reproduced in single copies by *scribes*, usually on vellum or parchment, using technological methods that were highly sophisticated for their time.

Marginalia. Scribbles, comments, and illustration written by the reader in the margin of a book.

Masoretic Signs. A type of musical notation for cantillation of the Masoretic Text, the authoritative text of the Hebrew Bible. The signs within the text indicate accents and tell the cantor how to sing each word. The signs appear in some medieval manuscripts of the Mishna.

Mass. The name used by the Catholic Church, Anglicans, Lutherans, and other Western branches of the church, for the sacrament of the Eucharist.

Matins. The Daily Office occurring during the night and ending at dawn. The night office was originally called *vigils* and was referenced that way by St. Benedict. The term *matins* was used to designate the morning office also known as *lauds*. *Vigils* and *matins* were combined and *matins* became the closing part of *vigils*, and *vigils* began to be observed at daybreak. By the time of the Council of Tours in 567, the night office was being called *matins*. It is the longest and most important Office of the day.

Mechanical Clock. Mechanical clocks came into use in Europe in the late 13th century. Water clocks had been in use prior to that time, but mechanical clocks driven by falling weights were made possible by the escapement mechanism. References to clocks increase significantly in church records throughout the medieval period.

Medieval Warm Period. A period of warm climate in the Northern Atlantic lasting from approximately 950 to 1250. The population of Europe exploded during this period.

Melismatic. Music in which multiple notes are sung to one syllable. *Contrast Syllabic.*

Melody. A succession of musical tones that the listener perceives as a coherent musical statement. Melody is often defined merely in terms of a succession of pitch and rhythm, but such definitions omit the necessary element of artistry and musical coherence. Melody is often used to describe the predominant voice in Western music, but that definition can be misleading when applied to music of the Middle Ages.

Membranophone. A classification of musical instruments in which a stretched membrane causes the vibration, e.g. drums. *Compare* Aerophones, Chordophones, Idiophones.

Mensural. Referring to music notation that indicates the measured durational value of notes. Mensural notation used a variety of note shapes to indicate durational values of notes in hierarchical numerical relation to each other. Notation was described by Franco of Cologne in his treatise *Ars cantus mensurabilis* (c. 1280).

Merovingian. Referring to the Merovingian Dynasty, which ruled the Frankish kingdom for almost 300 years. It was founded by Childeric I (457-481), the son of Merovec. Childeric's son Clovis I (481-511) united Gaul under Merovingian rule.

Metrical. Music or text that is arranged in a regular pattern of beats.

Metropolitan. Pertaining to the diocesan bishop or archbishop of a metropolis. The title is used in both Eastern and Western churches, but the rank of a metropolitan relative to other offices varies depending on the branch of the church. In Slavic Orthodox churches, a metropolitan ranks above an archbishop.

Mikveh. A bath used in Judaism for ritual immersion. The Mikveh has a complex history and set of uses. At the Temple, it was used by all Jews who wished to enter the precincts of the Sanctuary as a form of spiritual purification. It is used in the Jewish conversion process and by women prior to their wedding and at other regular intervals.

Miniature. A picture (illustraton) in an ancient medieval illuminated manuscript. The term is derived from the Latin *minium* (red lead) or *miniare* (to paint red) because decorations in early codices used that pigment. Similar terms in Latin indicate smallness: *minor, minimus, minutus*.

Miniscule. A script that became standard in Europe in Carolingian times, also called Carolingian miniscule. It was highly legible with rounded letters, clear capitals, and spaces between words. It has been attributed to Alcuin of York, although his personal involvement in the development of the script is disputed.

Mishna (Mishnah). The Mishna is a redaction of the Jewish oral traditions known as the Oral Torah by Rabbi Yehuda HaNasi before his death in 217 A.D. The oral law contained the traditions of Judaism and judgments of legal cases, giving guidance to the application of the law in everyday life. Before the destruction of the Temple in 70 A.D. it was prohibited to write down the oral law, but afterwards, without the Temple to serve as the center of Jewish study, it was necessary to put it in writing to preserve it.

Mnemonic. Aiding or designed to aid the memory. A mnemonic device is any learning technique that helps one memorize or retain information.

Mode. A way or manner in which something occurs or is done. Musical modes use the terminology associated with ancient Greek scales: Dorian, Phrygian, Lydian, Mixolydian. The modes for Gregorian chant retain that terminology but have different meanings. A medieval mode was generally determined by its "final" note (the one to which it progresses) and its "reciting tone" (the one around which the melody is centered).

Monastery. A building or complex of buildings occupied by a community of monks living under a religious rule.

Monk. One who practices religious asceticism living alone or in community with others. Hermitic monks are those who live in isolation from society. Early hermitic monks lived alone in huts or caves, a prime example being desert monks such as St. Anthony. Cenobitic monks live in a community (*monastery*). St. Pachomius (292-348) is generally thought of as the father of cenobitc monasticism.

Monody. The term is sometimes used as a substitute for monophony. It also refers to music of the 16th century and later in which a single, more soloistic melodic line is accompanied by instruments.

Monophonic. Consisting of a single musical line without accompaniment. The principal example of monophony is plainchant, consisting of a single melodic line sung by one person or by multiple singers in unison. *Contrast Polyphonic*.

Monotheism. Belief in the existence of one God. It is defined more specifically as belief in one personal and transcendent God.

Morphological. Having to do with the study of structure and form.

Mosaic. The art of creating an image with small pieces of colored glass, stone, or other materials. Mosaics were popular in ancient Greece and Rome and were employed when the building of early Christian churches began under Constantine. Ravenna, as the capital of the Western Empire in late Roman times, became the center of mosaic art. Use of the form in the West gradually declined after the fall of Rome but remained a prominent feature in Byzantium.

Motet. Generally, a piece of music in several parts with words, the term applies to various types of works in different eras. The earliest motets arose in the 13th century out of the Notre Dame School of organum. Upper voices were added to strophic interludes within longer sequences of organa. The effect was a rhythmic interlude within the more chant-like organum. Secular motets were later created with a different text in each voice (often in the vernacular) over a Latin *cantus firmus*. The *cantus firmus* was frequently played on instruments rather than sung.

Mozarabic. The Mozarabs were Christians who lived under Islamic rule in al-Andalus (Muslim Spain). The Mozarabic Rite, however, has roots that predate the Muslim invasion. Christian liturgy was in the Iberian Peninsula prior to the arrival of the Visigoths. The Mozarabic Rite thus more accurately refers to the liturgy practiced by visigothic Christians that was given its final form by St. Isidore of Seville in the 7th century. Christians who lived under Muslim rule after the invasion continued to use the rite.

Musica humana. One of the three divisions of music described by Boethius in *De Musica*. Music created by the human body.

Musica instrumentalis. One of the three divisions of music described by Boethius in *De Musica*. Music created by something under tension (strings, wind, water, or percussion).

Musica mundana. One of the three divisions of music described by Boethius in *De Musica*. Sometimes referred to as music of the spheres *or musica universalis*, it is the inaudible music resulting from the proportion and harmony of the celestial bodies.

Nave. The central part of the church intended to accommodate the congregation, extending from the entrance to the transepts. It is space intended for the laity.

Neume. A notational symbol predating the musical staff that indicates the basic contour and direction of a melodic phrase. Neumes did not indicate specific pitches but served more a memory aid for singers who were already familiar with the melody. Neumes appear in manuscripts from the 9th century.

Nomadic. Roaming about from place to place with no fixed pattern of movement.

Nomina sacra. Abbreviations in New Testament texts that were not used for economy, but to set certain holy words apart. Frequently the abbreviation was comprised of the first and last letter of the word, e.g. θc for θεóc (Theos).

None. The Daily Office occurring in mid-afternoon (the 9th hour).

Notation. Any system of written symbols used to represent aurally perceived music.

Notre Dame School. The group of composers working at or near the Notre Dame Cathedral in Paris from about 1160-1250 and the music they produced. The two principal composers are Léonin and Pérotin as reported in the writings of Anonymous IV.

Nun. A member of a religious community of women living under a rule; the female equivalent of a *monk*.

Oblique Motion. Melodic motion in which one voice stays on the same pitch while the other either rises or descends.

Ode. A poem expressing a strong feeling of love or respect for someone or something;

Offices. The canonical prayers recited daily by priests and monastics. The Daily Offices came from the Jewish practice of reciting prayers at set times of day. As monasticism spread, certain forms and prayers were standardized, notably by St. Benedict.

Old Believers. A branch of Orthodoxy that separated from the official Russian Orthodox Church as a protest against reforms introduced in 1666 by Patriarch Nikon of Moscow. Older practices were retained, including the excusive use of *znamenny* chant.

Opera. A staged dramatic work combining text and a musical score. The name is derived from *oper* meaning simply "work." The earliest opera still in the standard repertoire, called a *dramma per musica* (drama with music), is the 1607 work *Orfeo* by Claudio Monteverdi.

Opus Dei. The Divine Office; the "work" of the monks. *See Offices.*

Oral Transmission. The transmission of cultural materials and traditions in speech or song without the use of written materials.

Ordinary. The Ordinary of the Mass refers to the parts of the Mass that do not change for the specific occasion or from season to season within the Liturgical Year.

Ordinary Time. The long period of time in the Liturgical Year occurring after Pentecost and lasting until Advent (the beginning of the new Liturgical Year).

Organ. A musical instrument that produces sound by driving pressurized wind through pipes. The earliest organ was the *hydraulis* in which the air was pressurized by water. The introduction of organs into medieval churches is attributed to Pope Vitalian in the 7th century.

Organum. The early polyphony of the Middle Ages in which an additional voice was added to the chant, usually moving in parallel motion with the chant melody at the interval of a perfect fourth or fifth. The added voice (organal voice) was initially improvised. The 12th-century organum of St. Martial in Limoges was characterized by long melismas or "florid" organum. Organum of the Notre Dame School of composers was characterized by the use of rhythmic modes.

Ornamentation. Musical flourishes that are not necessary to carry the overall line of the melody (e.g. trills and grace notes), but which are added for interest frequently through improvisation.

Orthodox. Literally bearer of the right or true belief. The "Orthodox Church" usually refers to the various branches of the Eastern Orthodox Church with roots in Byzantium. Orthodox is also applied in other religious contexts to refer to branches of Christianity or Judaism that adhere to accepted norms or creeds.

Otche Nash. Transliteration of "Our Father" (Отче Наш) in Russian.

Pagan. A term originating in late Antiquity to refer to religions other than Judaism and Christianity. It generally implies a worldview that is pantheistic, polytheistic, or animistic.

Palaeography. The study of ancient and historical handwriting, the forms and processes of writing.

Pange lingua. "Sing my tongue." Hymn by St. Thomas Aquinas typically sung on Maundy Thursday as the Blessed Sacrament is carried out of the church.

Papyrologist. One who studies ancient literature and documents preserved in manuscripts written on papyrus.

Papyrus. Paper-like material made from the pith of the papyrus plant. Its first known use was by the ancient Egyptians.

Paradigm. An example, serving as a model or pattern.

Paragraphos. A horizontal stroke near the left margin of the page that was both decorative and functional. It separated sections of text and is the root of the English word "paragraph."

Parallel Motion. Melodic motion in which two voices rise and descend together, keeping the same interval between them.

Parchment. Material made from processed animal skin and used for writing. It was the material commonly used in medieval manuscripts until being replaced by paper around the end of the 15th century.

Pastoral. Pertaining to the keeping and grazing of sheep or cattle. In art, the term refers to an idealized depiction of country life and the herding of livestock.

Patrician. The ruling class of ancient Rome. The first one hundred men appointed by Romulus as senators were called "fathers" (*patres*), and their descendants became patricians.

Patristic. Pertaining to the early Church Fathers and their writings; the study of the writings of the Church Fathers.

Pax Romana. "Roman peace," referring to the time from the accession of Caesar Augustus in 27 B.C. to the death of Marcus Aurelius in 180 A.D. It was an era of relative peace after the Civil Wars of the Roman Republic and before the Crisis of the Third Century.

Pentecost. The occasion of the descent of the Holy Spirit on the apostles and followers of Christ described in Acts 2:1-31. From the Greek word for "fiftieth day," Pentecost occurs on the 50th day after Easter. In the Jewish calendar, Pentecost or *Shavuot* (weeks) marks the end of the 49-day Feast of Weeks (*see* Leviticus 23: 15-16) and is the day Jews traditionally celebrate the giving of the Torah to the nation of Israel on Mount Sinai.

Peregrinus. In Latin, a foreigner, one from abroad. The term was used in the Roman Empire to refer to a free subject who was not a citizen. St. Augustine in *The City of God* describes Christians as *peregrini,* citizens of the City of God who are having to pass through the City of Man.

Perfect Rhythm. Rhythm in which the predominant division of the beat is ternary.

Philological. Referring to the study of language in written historical sources.

Pietà. Christian art, usually sculpture, depicting the Virgin Mary cradling the dead body of Jesus.

Plague. See "Black Death."

Plainchant. From *cantus planus*, a 13th-century name for Gregorian chant, the term is used generically for the ancient style of monophonic and rhythmically free melody common to the various Western and Eastern Christian liturgies.

Plebian. Of the common people. The common people of ancient Rome, specifically the body of free citizens who were not *Patricians.*

Polyphonic. Consisting of multiple musical parts sung or played simultaneously. It generally applies to music in which two or more parts each have melodic interest and some rhythmic independence from one another. *Contrast Monophonic.*

Polytheism. The belief in or worship of multiple gods.

Portative Organ. From the Latin word for "carry," the portative organ consisted of one rank of pipes and was sufficiently small and light-weight to be carried by the performer in processions. It was highly popular in the 13th to 16th centuries.

Positive Organ. A small organ usually with one keyboard that is contained in a single chest that is relatively mobile. It differs from the portative organ in that it had a keyboard with more notes and was not carried on a sling by the performer.

Precentor. Derived from the Latin *præcentor* meaning "one who sings before," the precentor was normally the lead chanter who intoned certain parts of the service and gave the pitches to the bishop or other clergy. The title was often assigned to the person who taught the choir or acted as director of the *schola.*

Presentational Manuscript. A manuscript designed for presentation as a gift, often commissioned to be of an especially high quality.

Prime. The Daily Office occurring at the beginning of the day or about 6 a.m. (the first hour).

Proper. The proper of the Mass refers to the parts of the Mass that change according to the specific occasion or from season to season within the Liturgical Year.

Provenance. The beginning and course of something's existence. The record of ownership of a work of art used as a guide to its authenticity or quality. The provenance of a manuscript may be determined from marks or inscriptions within the manuscript, including clues as to who has owned, handled, revised, or read the manuscript and where it has been kept.

Quem quaeritis. Latin for "Whom do you seek?" – the question asked by the angel in the empty tomb to the three Marys on Easter morning. It became the focus of liturgical dramas in the 10th century.

Quire. *See Gathering.*

Relic. A part of a deceased person's body or belongings kept as an object of reverence.

Reconquista. The long series of battles between the Christians and Muslims on the Iberian Peninsula from 718 to 1492, resulting eventually in the Christians recapturing the territory from the Muslims.

Renaissance. Literally "rebirth," the period of European history between the 14th and 17th centuries that was marked by a renewed interest in classical influences and a flowering of the arts and scientific inquiry.

Rhetoric. The art of effective and persuasive speaking or writing. Rhetoric is one of the seven liberal arts.

Rhythmic Mode. An early manifestation of metrical rhythm in polyphonic music, the Notre Dame School defined six different patterns (modes) of long and short note values. One of these modes would predominate in the organal (upper) voice.

Romanesque. A form of medieval architecture characterized by semi-circular arches and massive walls with small windows.

Rorate caeli. From Isaiah 45:8: "Rorate caeli désuper et nubes pluant justum" (Drop down ye heavens from above, and let the clouds rain down the just.) The text is associated with Advent and with the Expectation of the Blessed Virgin Mary.

Rotunda. A building with a circular ground plan and often covered by a dome. It can also refer to a round room within a structure (e.g. the Rotunda in the U.S. Capitol). The rotunda had been used in Roman architecture and was used by Constantine for construction of the Church of the Holy Sepulcher. It remained a popular form of architecture in churches through the Middle Ages.

Royal Doors. The double doors in the center of the iconostasis. The Royal Doors (or Holy Doors) signify Christian continuity with the veil of the Temple that separated the people from the Holy of Holies. *Compare Deacons' Doors.*

Rule. A basic guide for living the Christian life in a community of monks or nuns. The Rule of St. Benedict, for example, prescribes the daily prayers and rules for the administration of the monastery.

Sacrament. From the Latin *sacramentum* (sign of the sacred). The outward and visible sign of an inward and spiritual grace. The medieval church recognized seven sacraments: the Eucharist, Baptism, Reconciliation, Confirmation, Marriage, Holy Orders, and Anointing of the Sick.

Sacrifice. The offering of food, objects, or the lives of animals to God as an act of propitiation or worship.

Sanctorale. The smaller of the two cycles of the Liturgical year, it consists of the fixed days of the feasts of the saints. *Compare Temporale.*

Sanctus. Meaning "holy," the Sanctus is part of the Ordinary of the Mass at the beginning of the Eucharist. Its text is taken from Isaiah 6:3 and Revelation 4:8.

Sarum. Old Sarum is the site of the earliest settlement in Salisbury, England. The Sarum Rite refers to the liturgy that was developed in Salisbury. It became prevalent in England until it was largely abandoned after the Protestant Reformation.

Schism. The split or division of opposing parties caused by differences in opinion or belief. A split within the Church. The Great Schism (or East-West Schism) of 1054 divided the Western or Roman Church under the pope from the Eastern or Orthodox Church centered in Byzantium.

Schola. A school or place of learning. A *schola cantorum* was the music school attached to a monastery or church. The term is used today for ensembles specializing in liturgical music.

Scribe. A person who writes books or documents by hand; a monk who copied manuscripts to create multiple copies for distribution.

Scriptio continua. The practice common in Greek papyri of writing with no spaces between words.

Scriptorium. A place for writing, usually referring to the rooms in monasteries where monks would sit making copies of manuscripts.

Scroll. A roll of papyrus, parchment, or paper containing writing.

Second Temple. The Temple in Jerusalem built c. 516 B.C. after the Babylonian Exile. The Second Temple was greatly expanded by King Herod over several decades beginning c. 20 B.C. It was destroyed by the Romans under Titus in 70 A.D.

Semitic. Pertaining to the family of languages that includes Hebrew, Arabic, and Aramaic. Referring to peoples who speak the Semitic languages.

Septuagint. The primary translation into Greek of the Hebrew scriptures dating from the 3rd century B.C.

Sepulcher (sepulchre). A small room or monument cut in a rock or built of stone as a place for burial; a tomb.

Seraphim. Described in Isaiah 6:1-8 as six-winged beings who fly around the throne of God crying "holy, holy, holy."

Sext. The Daily Office occurring at noon (the 6th hour).

Shema (Sh'ma). *Sh'ma Yisrael* are the first two words of the Jewish prayer that encapsulates monotheism: "Hear, O Israel: the Lord our God, the Lord is one." [Deuteronomy 6:4]

Shofar. An ancient musical instrument made of horn, usually that of a ram, used for religious purposes in Judaism.

Shrine. A site dedicated to a particular deity, martyr, or saint at which they are venerated or worshipped.

Silk Road. A ancient system of trade routes connecting East and West from the Mediterranean to China.

Solmization. The system of assigning syllables to each note in the musical scale or hexachord as an aid to sightsinging. *Solfège* or *Solfeggio* denotes the system prevalent in Europe that was derived from the first syllable of each phrase in the Hymn to St. John (*Ut quaent laxis*), attributed to Paul the Deacon. Each phrase began one step higher than the previous one, resulting in the syllables *ut, re, mi, fa, sol, la*.

Spondee. A metrical foot in poetry comprised of two stressed syllables, e.g. "Cry, cry! Troy burns."

Staff. The set of lines and spaces that represent pitch in musical notation. The staff allowed the representation of specific pitches and was a significant advancement over the imprecise pitch data conveyed by neumes.

Stained Glass. Glass colored by adding metallic salts during manufacture. Small pieces of glass were arranged to form patterns or pictures. The art form reached its height in the Middle Ages and was used to depict biblical narratives and saints' lives.

Stichometric Notes. These appear at the end of a text and indicate the number of lines the scribe has written, and thus how much to charge the commissioner.

Stoa. A covered walkway or portico for public use, usually with columns lining the side of buildings. The Royal Stoa in the Second Temple is an example.

Summa Theologica. The best-known work by Thomas Aquinas, it was intended as an instructional guide for theology students. It has been described as one of the classics of the history of philosophy and one of the most influential works of Western literature.

Syllabic. Music in which a syllable of text is given only one note. *Contrast Melismatic*.

Synagogue. A building where a Jewish congregation meets for worship. Synagogues are consecrated spaces used for prayer, reading, study, and assembly. They arose among diaspora Jews who were unable to worship in the Temple in Jerusalem.

Syncopation. A shifting of the accent in music to a beat that is normally unstressed. A displacement of the regular metrical accent.

Talmud. A central text of rabbinic Judaism. It has two components: the Mishna and the Gemara. Talmud may refer either to the Gemara alone or the Gemara and Mishna together. The Gemara, written in the three centuries following redaction of the Mishna, contains legal analysis and discussion of the Mishna. *See Mishna.*

Temporale. The larger of the two cycles of the Liturgical year, it consists of the movable feasts (also known as the Proper of the Time) that are focused on the life of Christ. Most movable feasts are tied to the date of Easter (e.g. Lent, Ascension, and Pentecost), which varies each year based on the cycle of the moon. Christmas and Advent are part of the Temporale although Christmas occurs on a fixed date. *Compare Sanctorale.*

Tenere. Latin for "to hold." The *cantus firmus* in early polyphony was often drawn out in long notes with faster moving upper voices or voices. From this derivation, the voice that sang the *cantus firmus* and "held" the chant became called the "tenor" and the higher voice above it the "altus."

Terce. The Daily Office occurring in mid-morning (the 3rd hour).

Tetrarchy. A form of government in which power is divided among four individuals. Diocletian established the Tetrarchy in the Roman Empire in 293, which ended the Crisis of the Third Century. It was comprised of two Augusti, one for East and one for West, and two Caesars who would serve under the Augusti. The Tetrarchy initially consisted of Diocletian as Augustus in the East, Maximian as Augustus in the West, Galerius as Caesar in the East, and Contantius as Caesar in the West.

Texture. How the layers of melodic, rhythmic, and harmonic, materials are combined in music, thus determining the overall quality of the sound of a work.

Theotokos. God-bearer; Mother of God. The term used in Eastern Orthodoxy to refer to the Holy Virgin Mary.

Three-Field Rotation. A system of crop rotation used in medieval Europe that allowed two-thirds of the land to be in use at all times while the remained third lay fallow. It replaced the two-field system in which half of the land was kept out of production.

Timbrel. A percussion instrument (idiophone) of the ancient Israelites similar to the tambourine.

Tonality. A musical system that arranges pitches or chords to induce a hierarchy of perceived relations, stabilities, and attractions. The tonal system of major and minor keys became the norm in the early baroque era, after about 1600. In contrast, music prior to that time is often classified according to modes, i.e. tonal vs. modal music.

Torah. The five books of Moses: Genesis, Exodus, Leviticus, Numbers, Deuteronomy. The Torah, meaning instruction or teaching, consists of the foundational narrative of the Jews and their religious and moral obligations.

Trecento. Italian for three hundred. Short for *mille trecento* meaning 1300, it refers to the 14th century in Italian cultural history.

Tribrach. A metrical foot in poetry comprised of the unstressed syllables.

Trochee. A metrical foot in poetry comprised of one stressed syllable followed by one unstressed syllable, e.g. "Double, double, toil and trouble."

Trope. From the Greek *tropos*: to turn or change. In medieval music it refers to something added to the pre-existing chant.

Troubadour. A French medieval lyric poet composing and singing in Provençal in the 11th to 13th centuries, especially on the theme of courtly love.

Vault. An arched structure forming a ceiling or roof; a space or room covered by an arched structure.

Vellum. Fine parchment made from calf skin as opposed to the skin of other animals.

Veneration. The act of honoring a saint. A type of honor distinct from the adoration due to God alone.

Vernacular. The language or dialect spoken by ordinary people in a particular country or region.

Vespers. The Daily Office occurring at sunset, from the Greek *hespera* and Latin *vesper* meaning "evening."

Vigil. The Night Office, sometimes sung as a part of *matins* although in some traditions it is observed separately. Vigil was originally composed of four "watches" spanning the entire time between sunset and daylight.

Vox organalis. A voice added to a plainchant melody (*vox principalis*) singing the same melody in parallel motion at a fixed interval.

Vox principalis. A plainchant melody to which an organal voice (*vox organalis*) is added to create *Organum*.

Vulgate. The 4th-century Latin translation of the Bible done primarily by St. Jerome. It was commissioned by Pope Damasus I to revise the *Vetus Latina* ("Old Latin") collection of texts, but the project expanded to become a complete Latin version of the Bible. It is credited with being the first Latin translation of Old Testament texts directly from the Hebrew. It was widely accepted as the *versio vulgata* (the "version commonly used") or simply *vulgata*.

Znak. Term used for a sign or symbol (neume) placed above a word of text in early Orthodox chant notation.

Znammeny. A singing tradition of melismatic, monophonic liturgical chant used in the Russian Orthodox Church.

Selected Bibliography

Adams, Jeremy. *The "Populus" of Augustine and Jerome: A Study in the Patristic Sense of Community*. New Haven: Yale University Press, 1971.

Aquilina, Mike. *The Fathers of the Church: An Introduction to the First Christian Teachers*. Expanded ed. Huntington: Our Sunday Visitor, 1994.

_____. *The Mass of the Early Christians*. 2d ed. Huntington: Our Sunday Visitor, 2007.

Bishop, Morris. *The Middle Ages*. New York: Houghton Mifflin, 1968.

Bonner, Gerald. *St. Augustine of Hippo: Life and Controversies*. 3d ed. Norwich: Canterbury Press, 2002.

Bradshaw, Paul F. *Reconstructing Early Christian Worship*. Collegeville, Mn: Liturgical Press, 2009.

Calhoun, David. *Ancient & Medieval Church History*. Audio Lectures. Covenant Theological Seminary, 2010. iTunes U.

Chesterton, G. K. *St. Thomas Aquinas*. New York: Sheed & Ward, 1933.

Dales, Douglas. *Alcuin: His Life and Legacy*. Cambridge: James Clarke, 2012.

Dmytryshyn, Basil, ed. *Medieval Russia: A Source Book, 900-1700*. 2d ed. New York: Holt, Reinhart, and Winston, 1973.

Drogan, Marc. *Medieval Calligraphy: Its History and Technique*. Montclair: Allanheld, Osmun, 1980.

Duffy, Eamon. *The Stripping of the Altars*. New Haven: Yale University Press, 1992.

Enslin, Morton Scott. *Christian Beginnings: Parts I and II*. New York: Harper, 1956.

Fletcher, Richard. *The Barbarian Conversion: From Paganism to Christianity*. Berkeley: University of California Press, 1997.

Freedman, Paul. *The Early Middle Ages, 284-1000*. Fall 2011. Yale University Open Course. http://oyc.yale.edu/history/hist-210

Goodman, Martin. *Rome and Jerusalem: The Clash of Ancient Civilizations.* London: Penguin, 2007.

Gradenwitz, Peter. *The Music of Israel: From the Biblical Era to Modern Times.* Portland: Amadeus, 1996.

Heer, Friedrich, *The Medieval World.* Trans. by Janet Sondheimer. New York: New American Library, 1961.

Holland, Tom. *Millennium.* London: Little, Brown, 2008.

Hourlier, Dom Jacques. *Reflections on the Spirituality of Gregorian Chant.* Rev. ed. Trans. by Dom Gregory Casprini and Robert Edmonson. Brewster, Mass: Paraclete Press, 2012.

Idelsohn, Abraham Z. *Jewish Music: Its Historical Development.* New York: Dover, 1992.

————. *Jewish Liturgy and its Development.* New York: Dover, 1995.

Jones, A. H. M. *Constantine and the Conversion of Europe.* London: English Universities Press, 1948.

Lorenz, Frederick. *Life of Alcuin.* Translated by Jane Mary Slee. London: Thomas Hurst, St. Paul's Church-Yard, 1837.

Marshner, William. "The Great Schism." January 2011. Christendom College. Extra-Campus Lectures. https://itunes.apple.com/us/itunes-u/off-campus/ id418586052?mt=10

Massie, Suzanne. *Land of the Firebird: The Beauty of Old Russia.* New York: Simon & Schuster, 1980.

McClure, M.L. and Charles Lett Feltoe. *The Pilgrimage of Etheria.* London: Macmillan, 1904.

McGuire. Brendan. "The Crusades." November 2008. Christendom College. Extra-Campus Lectures. https://itunes.apple.com/us/itunes-u/off-campus/ id418586052?mt=10

————. "Reconquista: Islam & Christianity at War." March 2009. Christendom College. Extra-Campus Lectures. https://itunes.apple.com/us/itunes-u/off-campus/ id418586052?mt=10

McKinnon, James, ed. *Music in Early Christian Literature.* Cambridge: Cambridge University Press, 1987.

O'Donnell, Timothy. "The Fall of Jerusalem." March 2010. Christendom College. Extra-Campus Lectures. https://itunes.apple.com/us/itunes-u/off-campus/id418586052?mt=10

Reese, Gustave. *Music in the Middle Ages.* New York: W. W. Norton, 1968.

Rowley H.H. *Worship in Ancient Israel: Its Forms and Meaning.* London: SPCK, 1967.

Scott, Robert A. *The Gothic Enterprise: A Guide to Understanding the Medieval Cathedral.* Berkeley: University of California Press, 2003.

Scruton, Roger. "Music and Morality." *American Spectator* (Feb. 2010). http://spectator.org/articles/40193/music-and-morality

Seay, Albert. *Music in the Medieval World.* Englewood Cliffs: Prentice-Hall, 1965.

Shoeman, Roy H. *Salvation Is from the Jews.* San Francisco: Ignatius Press, 2003.

Smith, L. M., *The Early History of the Monastery of Cluny.* London: Oxford University Press, 1920.

Strunk, Oliver, ed. *Source Readings in Music History: Antiquity and the Middle Ages.* New York: W. W. Norton, 1965.

Sypeck, Jeff. *Becoming Charlemagne: Europe, Baghdad, and the Empires of A.D. 800.* New York: Harper Collins, 2006.

Taruskin, Richard. *Oxford History of Western Music.* Oxford: Oxford University Press, 2005.

These Truths We Hold: The Holy Orthodox Church: Her Life and Teachings. A Monk of St. Tikhon's Monastery, ed. South Canaan, Pa: St. Tikhon's Seminary Press, 1992.

Trepp, Leo. *A History of the Jewish Experience: Eternal Faith, Eternal People.* New York: Behrman House, 1962.

Wheeler, Mortimer. *Roman Art and Architecture*. New York: Oxford University Press, 1964.

Wunsch, Paul. "Confessions of St. Augustine." September 2011. Christendom College. Extra-Campus Lectures. https://itunes.apple.com/us/itunes-u/off-campus/id418586052?mt=10

Appendix

ORDINARY OF THE MASS

Kyrie

Kyrie eleison	Lord, have mercy
Christe eleison	Christ, have mercy
Kyrie eleison	Lord, have mercy

Gloria

Gloria in excelsis Deo.
Et in terra pax
hominibus bonæ voluntatis.

Glory be to God in the highest.
And in earth peace
to men of good will.

Laudamus te; benedicimus te;
adoramus te; glorificamus te.
Gratias agimus tibi
propter magnam gloriam tuam.

We praise Thee; we bless Thee;
we worship Thee; we glorify Thee.
We give thanks to Thee
for Thy great glory.

Domine Deus, Rex coelestis,
Deus Pater omnipotens.
Domine Fili unigenite Jesu Christe.
Domine Deus, Agnus Dei,
Filius Patris.

O Lord God, Heavenly King,
God the Father Almighty.
O Lord Jesus Christ, the only
begotten Son.
Lord God, Lamb of God,
Son of the Father.

Qui tollis peccata mundi,
miserere nobis.
Qui tollis peccata mundi,
suscipe deprecationem nostram.
Qui sedes ad dextram Patris,
O miserere nobis.

Thou that takest away the sins of
the world,
have mercy upon us.
Thou that takest away the sins of
the world,
receive our prayer.
Thou that sittest at the right hand
of the Father,
have mercy upon us.

Quoniam tu solus Sanctus,

For thou only art holy,

tu solus Dominus,
tu solus Altissimus, Jesu Christe.
Cum Sancto Spiritu
in gloria Dei Patris.
Amen.

thou only art the Lord,
thou only art the most high, Jesus
Christ.
Together with the Holy Ghost
in the glory of God the Father.
Amen.

Credo

Credo in unum Deum, Patrem
omnipoténtem, factorem cæli et terræ,
visibílium ómnium et invisibílium.

I believe in one God, the Father
almighty, maker of heaven and
earth, of all things visible and
invisible.

Et in unum Dóminum Iesum Christum,
Fílium Dei unigénitum, et ex Patre natum,
ante ómnia sæcula. Deum de Deo, lumen
de lúmine, Deum verum de Deo vero,
génitum, non factum, consubstantiálem
Patri: per quem ómnia facta sunt. Qui
propter nos hómines et propter nostram
salútem descéndit de cælis. Et incarnátus
est de Spíritu Sancto ex María Vírgine, et
homo factus est. Crucifíxus étiam pro
nobis sub Póntio Piláto; passus et sepúltus
est, et resurréxit tértia die, secúndum
Scriptúras, et ascéndit in cælum, sedet ad
déxteram Patris. Et íterum ventúrus est
cum glória, iudicáre vivos et mórtuos,
cuius regni non erit finis.

And in one Lord Jesus Christ, the
Only Begotten Son of God, born of
the Father before all ages. God of
God, Light of Light, true God of true
God, begotten, not made, being of
one substance with the Father; by
whom all things were made. Who
for us men and for our salvation
came down from heaven, and was
incarnate of the Holy Ghost and of
the Virgin Mary, and was made
man; was crucified also for us
under Pontius Pilate, he suffered
and was buried, and the third day
rose again according to the
Scriptures. He ascended into
heaven and is seated at the right
hand of the Father. He will come
again in glory to judge the living
and the dead and his kingdom will
have no end.

Et in Spíritum Sanctum, Dóminum et
vivificántem: qui ex Patre Filióque
procédit. Qui cum Patre et Fílio simul
adorátur, et conglorificátur: qui locútus est
per Prophétas.

I believe in the Holy Spirit, the
Lord, the giver of life, who proceeds
from the Father and the Son, who
with the Father and the Son is to be
adored and glorified, who spoke by
the prophets.

Et unam, sanctam, cathólicam et apostólicam Ecclésiam. Confíteor unum baptísma in remissiónem peccatorum. Et expecto resurrectionem mortuorum, et vitam ventúri sæculi. Amen.

I believe in one, holy, catholic and apostolic Church. I confess one Baptism for the forgiveness of sins and I look forward to the resurrection of the dead and the life of the world to come. Amen.

Sanctus

Sanctus, Sanctus, Sanctus
Dominus Deus Sabaoth.
Pleni sunt caeli et terra gloria tua.
Hosanna in excelsis.

Holy, holy, holy, Lord God of Hosts:
heaven and earth are full of thy glory:
Hosanna, in the highest.

Benedictus qui venit in nomine Domini.
Hosanna in excelsis.

Blessed is he that commeth in the name of the Lord:
Glory to thee, O lord in the highest.

Agnus Dei

Agnus Dei, qui tollis peccata mundi, miserere nobis.

Lamb of God, that takest away the sins of the world, have mercy on us.

Agnus Dei, qui tollis peccata mundi, miserere nobis.

Lamb of God, that takest away the sins of the world, have mercy on us.

Agnus Dei, qui tollis peccata mundi, dona nobis pacem.

Lamb of God, that takest away the sins of the world, grant us peace.

DAILY OFFICES

Office	Original time	Typical time
Matins	Midnight	2-3 a.m.
Lauds	3 a.m.	2-3 a.m. (sung immediately after *matins*)
Prime	6 a.m.	Upon rising
Terce	9 a.m.	9 a.m.
Sext	Noon	Noon
None	3 p.m.	3 p.m.
Vespers	6 p.m.	At sunset
Compline	9 p.m.	Before bed